# Śrī
# Mahāprabhu

## His Life, Religion & Philosophy

by

**Svāmī Tapasyānanda**

**Sri Ramakrishna Math**
Mylapore, Madras 600 004

Published by
The President
Sri Ramakrishna Math
Mylapore, Chennai-4



IV-2M 3C-8-2002
ISBN 81-7120-259-4

Printed in India at
Sri Ramakrishna Math Printing Press
Mylapore, Chennai-4

## Preface

'*Bhakti Schools of Vedānta*', of which this volume is a part, is a work intended to bring to the notice of the general reader that it is not correct to equate Vedānta exclusively with Advaita Vedānta, associated with Śrī Śaṅkarācārya. There are several other Ācāryas who have expounded the Vedānta in quite a different way and whose status as teachers of Vedānta requires recognition.

The personages treated in the above book are Śrī Rāmānuja, Śrī Nimbārka, Śrī Vallabha, Śrī Madhva and Śrī Caitanya. Besides their theo-philosophies, detailed accounts of their lives are given. For it is the support of their lives that gives more authority to their teachings than the philosophical writings of mere armchair philosophers. The frame-work of their lives is mainly historical, but most of the miraculous and extraordinary incidents mentioned in them may largely be projections of the pious imaginations of their followers. These too are to be respectfully received and not pooh-poohed as mere cock and bull stories. It is the way of the Indian mind to convey the idea that these Ācāryas are endowed with extraordinary powers. But for this, their teachings could not have survived through so many centuries influencing the lives of innumerable generations of men.

For the benefit of those who cannot go in for the full volume at a time, the section dealing with each Ācārya is brought out as a separate book under the caption of their respective names. Śrī Caitanya is the theme of this book.

Sri Ramakrishna Math
Mylapore, Madras 600 004

Publishers

## KEY TO TRANSLITERATION AND PRONUNCIATION

| | | Sounds like | | | Sounds like |
|---|---|---|---|---|---|
| अ | a | o in son | ठ | th | th in ant-hill |
| आ | ā | a in master | ड | d | d in den |
| इ | i | i in if | ढ | dh | dh in godhood |
| ई | ī | ee in feel | ण | n | n in under |
| उ | u | u in full | त | t | t in French |
| ऊ | ū | oo in boot | थ | th | th in thumb |
| ऋ | r | somewhat between | द | d | th in then |
| | | r an ri | ध | dh | then in breathe |
| ए | e | ay in May | न | n | n in not |
| ऐ | ai | y in my | प | p | p in pen |
| ओ | o | o in oh | फ | ph | ph in loop-hole |
| औ | au | ow in now | ब | b | b in bag |
| क | k | k in keen | भ | bh | bh in abhor |
| ख | kh | ckh in blockhead | म | m | m in mother |
| ग | g | g (hard) in go | य | y | y in yard |
| घ | gh | gh in ghee | र | r | r in run |
| ङ | ṅ | ng in singer | ल | l | l in luck |
| च | c | ch (not k) chain | व | v | v in avert |
| छ | ch | chh in catch him | श | ś | sh in reich (German) |
| ज | j | j in judge | ष | ṣ | sh in show |
| झ | jh | dgeh in hedgehog | स | s | s in sun |
| ञ | ñ | n (somewhat) as in | ह | h | in hot |
| | | French | | ṁ | m in sum |
| ट | t | t tn ten | | h | h in half |

# Śrī Caitanya Mahāprabhu: Life

The life of Śrī Caitanya narrated here is mainly based on Jadunāth Sirkār's abridgement of Caitanya-caritāmṛta, the most authentic work on Caitanya by Kṛṣṇa Dās Kavirāj (1517-1582). He was a disciple of Raghunāth Dās, a contemporary and personal attendant of Caitanya during his life at Puri. Educated well in Sanskrit and Persian, Kṛṣṇa Dās left his home in Burdwan early in life and wandered towards Vṛndāvan, and settled at Rādhā-kuṇḍ about twelve miles away from Vṛndāvan proper. In his earlier years he wrote mostly in Sanskrit, but at the request of devotees he started writing his magnum opus in Bengali, a classic in that language, in his old age and completed it in 1581, one year before his demise.

Besides Jadunāth Sirkār's abridged translation of this great work, we have also drawn materials from the abridged edition of 'Lord Gaurānga' by Sisir Kumār Ghose, the well-known editor of Amritbasar Pattrika, wherein he has given a very interesting and illuminating account of Caitanya's early life, based on facts collected from other works in Bengali on this great incarnation.

**Early Life**

Śrī Caitanya (1486-1533) was born, on 4th February, a lunar eclipse day, at Māyāpur in the township of Navadvip, as the son of Jagannāth Miśra, a learned Paṇḍit of the place and his wife Śaci. Situated about 75 miles to the north of modern Calcutta on the bank of holy Gaṅgā in Nadia District, Navadvip of the 15th century was a prosperous town. It was a great centre of trade and equally of learning. What is called Navya-nyāya, the new system of logic, which had its birth in Mithila, had been introduced to Navadvip before this time. It was developed by a succession of great scholars, at the head of which stands Gaṅgeśa (about 1200 A.D.). Students from all over India flocked to Navadvip to learn Nyāya and get the impremature of some great scholar or institution of Navadvip. Such development of learning was also helped by the liberal patronage extended to students and professors by the prosperous society of Nadia.

Towards the 15th century, which witnessed the advent of Caitanya, Navadvip, though still reputed as a centre of learning, was without any spiritual lustre. Vaiṣṇavism was the religion professed, but the Paṇḍits in general were without spiritual ardour. Consumption of liquor and meat had become common among them with the development of Tantrism. Religion had degenerated into mere rituals, and the intellectualism of the Paṇḍits was spent in acrimonious and demonstrative debates punctuated with feasting and frivolous entertainments. Devotion to God, which is the important teaching of Vaiṣṇavism, found no place in their lives. Stricken to the core of his heart by this decline of Bhakti and ascendency of materialism, Advaita Ācārya, a learned man and a genuine Vaiṣṇava devotee of the Lord, used always to pray to Kṛṣṇa "O Lord! if Thou dost incarnate Thyself, then only these creatures will find redemption". It is said that it was in response to the prayers of this devotee that Caitanya appeared on earth.

In the family of Jagannāth Paṇḍita and Śaci, Caitanya was the tenth child to be born. Eight daughters and a boy had preceded him. All the eight daughters died in infancy while the boy Viśveśvara happened to leave hearth and home at the early age of sixteen and take to the wandering life of an itinerant monk. Though the new born boy, the tenth in the family, was given the name of Viśvambhara by his father in the light of his horoscope, his mother Śaci named him Nimāi, a word meaning 'short lived' and reminiscent of the bitter taste of the fruit and leaves of Neem tree. She did so because of the belief that such an undesirable association with the name would avert possible dangers from the evil influences that had caused the loss of all her earlier issue. Some say that this name was given to him because he was born under a neem tree. His name was changed in recognition of his beauty into Gaurāṅga (the golden-coloured one) at the time of investiture with the sacred thread, and again into Śrī Kṛṣṇa Caitanya (he who awakens God in the hearts of men) by the spiritual teacher who initiated him into Sannyāsa later.

His life as an infant and as a child was very much reminiscent of that of Śrī Kṛṣṇa himself. It is said that the beaming beauty of the infant was so attractive that the women who came to see him fondled him and passed him from hand to hand, leaving little time for his mother to attend to him. It was found the utterance of the name of Hari pacified him whenever he was crying. When he began to crawl he was often found proceeding to the streets, so much so that he had to be constantly watched. This became all the more so when he began to walk. One day he was found to have caught a cobra. Another day he walked into the street with jewellery adorning his body and fell into the hands of a thief who tried to carry him to his den. But wonder of wonders! The thief lost his way as he proceeded and found himself at Nimāi's house. The experience had a miraculous effect on the thief, who turned into an ascetic and lived the life of a holy man thereafter. This was the beginning of miraculous conversions in Caitanya's life.

Nimāi's beauty was exquisite. His complexion rivalled the brilliance of molten gold. His palms and the soles of his feet looked as if they were painted with vermilion. His lips were ruddy like Bimba fruit, and his eyes were most lovely, elongated like lotus petals and moist as it were with lotus honey.

Many supernatural phenomena were seen manifesting on the boy's body. While sleeping a moonlike aura was sometimes found floating over him and in his bed room many luminous figures appeared before his mother. Once when the mother asked him to go to the next room where his father was seated, both the parents heard the sounds of anklet worn by children, as Nimāi was walking. This was interpreted as an indication of the presence of Gopāla in him. But all this only raised fears in the mind of mother Śaci, who felt that they presaged some evil to her beloved Nimāi.

As he grew up he began to indulge in many pranks like boy Kṛṣṇa, delighting the hearts of people. In the play field he would lose himself in play forgetful even of food, and only the tears of his mother would bring him back home. Restless by nature, he often ran out of his house to those of others and asked for whatever he saw, be it fried rice, bananas or sweets. Every one gave him with pleasure whatever he asked for. Sometimes he took liberties in others' houses, by stealthily drinking their milk, or eating their rice and other edibles. When he found nothing to eat he would break their utensils. If caught redhanded, he would implore in a very winning manner. "Let me off this time. I shall not come here again to steal." None felt angry with him. Only they marvelled at his cleverness and his very attractive poses.

He was given to dancing with companions, chanting Hari's name with hands uplifted. Once this impromptu dance became so exciting and thrilling that an old and learned passerby was caught up in that devotion-charged atmosphere and joined the group of boys who were dancing with Nimāi in the centre.

The boy began to develop traits of character that seemed shocking to his parents. They were orthodox

Brāhmaṇas and mother Śaci observed the caste rules strictly. The boy would tease her by violating them, but when criticised by his mother for this, his reply was: "The idea of external purity is a delusion." If the angry mother took a rod in hand to punish him for his wilful breach of caste rules, the boy would run into unclean places where the mother would not dare to go. Much worse, he would touch a Chamar, an untouchable, and threaten to pollute the mother by touching her in his supposedly unclean state. This would make Śaci run indoors.

Certain unusual signs of divinity also began to manifest in him. Śaci, in consultation with old matrons of the village, believed that Nimāi was possessed by some evil spirit and that offerings made to the goddess Ṣaṣṭi could save him from the grip of these spirits. The mother prepared the offerings and was taking them to the temple of the goddess. Nimāi suddenly appeared before her and demanded the food to satisfy his excruciating hunger, and snatched it away from the mother. When he was about five, he began to cry one day in utter distraction. Nothing would pacify him. When finally questioned about what he wanted, he replied, "I want the offerings which Jagadīṣ and Hiraṇya have prepared for God." A shocking demand indeed! The two persons mentioned were pious Brāhmaṇas who, after observing Ekādaśi by fasting, had prepared some offerings to be made to Kṛṣṇa, before they broke their fast. How did the boy know of it, and more so how could he demand it? The two Brāhmaṇas came to know of this, and hastened to see what the matter was. Strangely they felt that Śrī Kṛṣṇa had entered into the boy and was demanding the food. They therefore brought the offerings and fed Nimāi as Bāla-Gopāla. In later years they became the ardent followers of Caitanya.

A still more wonderful conversion was that of a hard-baked Advaitin, named Murāri Gupta, who was an adept in the highly philosophical and abstract text

Yogavāsiṣṭha. Young Nimāi often made fun at his expense mimicking his gestures and pedantic postures while he expounded the text to ardent listeners. "What a perverted child you are!" remarked Murāri, which provoked from the Nimāi the threat "I shall teach you a lesson at dinner time." One day while Murāri was at his meal, Nimāi suddenly appeared and fouled his dish. Murāri was stunned at this. When he recovered from his stupor, he heard the child telling, 'O Murāri, give up your false and dangerous doctrine that you are one with the Almighty God. Giving up these pretensions, worship Śrī Kṛṣṇa." This had a wonderful effect on Murāri. Next day he went to the house of Jagannāth Miśra, and prostrated himself before Nimāi. At this the parents got frightened that such an adoration of him by a learned Brāhmaṇa might bring evil on Nimāi.

## Education and Life as a Professor

When Nimāi was about seven his elder brother Viśveśvar, then sixteen years old, took to the life of an ascetic and left his hearth and home, leaving his parents in great sorrow for what was in effect a bereavement. This brought about more seriousness in Nimāi too. He had refused to attend any Tol (Sanskrit school) till then. Now he began to study and made very rapid progress, as he was a Śrutidhara — one who could grasp and remember anything by hearing once. At nine he was invested with the sacred thread and admitted to the performance of Vedic duties. His father, who was himself a great Paṇḍit, was glad at this, but his joy was short-lived, as he passed away soon after, stricken by an incurable fever. Mother Śaci was now the boy's sole guardian and the head of the family. She took care to see that Nimāi got the best education possible and put him under the tuition of Paṇḍit Gaṅgādās, a person of impeccable character and unrivalled scholarship. Soon Nimāi distinguished himself as the best pupil under the Paṇḍit, and trounced in debate talented fellow-students like Kamala Kānta, Kṛṣṇānanda and Murāri Gupta. Catching the debate-fever of Nadia Paṇḍịts, he began to go to neighbouring places challenging scholars of established reputation. At this early age he wrote a work on grammar which got recognition even in that place noted for learning. Having mastered literature and gràmmar, he now turned to the study of logic under the very reputed scholar Vāsudeva Sārvabhauma. Soon he excelled all his fellow students including Raghunātha, who had already written a very authoritative text on Nyāya called Didhīti. Sārvabhauma, asked this particular student to analyse a knotty logical fallacy. It took him a whole day to give the right answer. The same problem was given to Nimāi, who did it on the spot in a flash. Raghunātha came to learn from Nimāi that the latter was writing a work on Nyāya. As he himself was writing one in the hope that it would be hailed as the best work on the subject, he was anxious to know how Nimāi's work would stand in comparison with his own. So while they both were crossing the river in a boat to their Master's Tol, Raghunāth wanted to hear some pages of Nimāi's book read. As Nimāi read it, Raghunāth's face became morose and he burst into tears, because of the feeling that his ambition would be defeated utterly in the face of Nimāi's work. To pacify and gladden his friend, Nimāi, without the slightest hesitation, threw away his work into the Gaṅgā, so that his friend's ambition might not go in vain. Thus the world lost a master-piece of Nyāya, but got a Master in compensation.

At sixeen Nimāi started a Tol of his own. Though the youngest professor in Nadia, his widening reputation for learning attracted large numbers of students to his institution. At about this time he married Lakṣmī, the daughter of a noted Nyāya Paṇḍit, Vallabhācārya. Unlike the other Paṇḍits, Nimai continued to entertain his jovial and boyish mood even after he had settled down to a scholarly profession. Though strikingly handsome and reputed for intelligence, he remained playful as ever, and swam, ran up and down the streets, and played with his students, many of whom were much older than himself.

Somehow, teasing Vaiṣṇavas was one of his hobbies at this time. Once a well-known person named Mukunda, who was trying to avoid Nimāi for this reason, was however confronted by the latter with the remark, "You avoid me, because you take me to be an infidel. In time I too shall become a Vaiṣṇava but not a humbug like you." Śrīvas, a close friend of his father, once advised him to join the Vaiṣṇavas and lead them by living an exemplary life. Nimāi gave the mock-serious reply: "Well, respected sir, I have become a Professor at this early age. Let me enjoy my triumphs for some time, and when I am tired, I shall consider your suggestion."

And so he continued his life of teaching the ever-increasing number of students gathering at his Tol, and challenging other scholars to debates. He now went on a scholarly tour of eastern districts to challenge the Paṇḍits in those regions. His fame had already preceded him. He therefore received a red carpet welcome wherever he went. One notable event surprising Nimāi and others was the adoration given to him by an elderly Brāhmaṇa devotee Tapan Miśra. Miśra made his way to Nimāi and fell at his feet saying that a Divine voice had asked him to seek refuge in Nimāi Paṇḍit who was no other than the Lord manifest on earth for the salvation of sinners. Tapan Miśra seems to be the first one to recognise him as an incarnation.

When Nimāi returned home after one year's victorious tour, he found that his wife Lakṣmī had died of snake bite. He, however, continued his life of teaching, attracting many students and handsome donations from patrons. All the income that came, he never appropriated for himself. It went to his mother who was the mistress of the household. About this time a great scholar named Keśava came to Nadia challenging all the Paṇḍits there. One moonlit night Keśava happened to meet Nimāi, whom he treated in a condescending way. Nimāi received this insult submissively. As a topic for exchange of thought Nimāi requested Keśava to describe the glories of the holy river Gaṅgā in a poem. Without any effort the latter composed a hundred grand verses in a short time to the surprise and admiration of all. Nimāi however wanted him to analyse one verse and expound its beauty. On being asked to select one, Nimāi recited one verse from the middle, which he had heard only once, and showed five blemishes in it on the basis of the accepted rules of poetics. The 'world-conqueror', as Keśava called himself, had to eat the humble pie. It is said that the humiliated Keśava had that night a consoling dream in which Sarasvati revealed to him that Nimāi was Kṛṣṇa himself.

The defeat of Keśava left Nimāi as the unrivalled scholar in all that region. His mother felt her beloved son had achieved all that life could offer. Only he lacked a wife, and she soon managed to overcome this deficiency by getting Nimāi married to Viṣṇupriyā, the daughter of a wealthy and reputed Paṇḍit of the place.

**Visit to Gaya and Transformation**

It was not long after his victory tour of East Bengal that he undertook a pilgrimage to Gaya, to perform the Piṇḍa or obsequies for the salvation of his ancestors. This was a turning point in his life. After the Piṇḍa rites, when he worshipped at Viṣṇu-pāda, the shrine of the Deity Gadādhara, a strange mood came over him and he fell into a trance. In that trance he was about to fall down when he was supported from behind by an ascetic Īśvara Purī, disciple of Mādhavendra Purī, a celebrated personage who was the first to introduce the practice of Bhakti among Sannyāsins. Nimāi had had a casual acquaintance with Īśvara Purī even at Nadia. As soon as Nimāi came to his normal consciousness, he requested Purī, to his surprise, to help him realise a glimpse of Rādhā's love for Śrī Kṛṣṇa. Purī initiated him into the Mantra for Kṛṣṇa-worship — a Mantra which means salutation to Kṛṣṇa, the Beloved of the Gopis. Nimāi was immediately transformed. His jovial mood disappeared, giving place to one of inexpressible sorrow and inner pathos. Repeated surges of longing for Kṛṣṇa, followed by a sense of the calm of fulfilment, tossed his soul from sorrow to ecstasy and from ecstasy to sorrow. His students who had accompanied him found him reluctant to return to Nadia. He longed to go immediately to Vrndāvan to meet Kṛṣṇa. Somehow they persuaded him to go back to see his mother. He agreed and returned in a completely changed mood of abstraction.

Gone were his mirth and intellectual aggressiveness. He appeared to be the weakest of the weak. He would speak of nothing but Kṛṣṇa. At Suklāmber's house he fell down in a trance uttering "My Kṛṣṇa!" and when he regained his senses, he touched his heart and blabbered, "I captured my Kṛṣṇa, but he has fled. There is a void in the heart and the whole world cannot fill it. Will no one bring Him back to me!"

Now as a measure to bring him back to normalcy, his old teacher Gaṅgādās asked him to re-open his Tol. He did so, but he could not teach as before. When he opened his book uttering "Hari" as usual, he fell into a trance. For a few days he tried to take classes, but what he talked would be only on Kṛṣṇa and not on the subject for study. At last he asked his students to excuse him for wasting their time. He continued "My friends, as soon as I begin my lessons, an exquisitely beautiful boy of dark complexion comes and stands before me, playing on a flute. The sight of him takes away my senses and I forget everything else. It is no longer within my power to teach as I used to. Allow me to take leave of you all." But they would not go. Nimāi then proposed to have a Kṛṣṇa-Kīrtan and all joined in the dance and choral singing of "Salutations to Kṛṣṇa! Salutations to Hari!" There began to flow a river of Bhakti and the crowd was, as it were, soon swimming in it.

**Self-Revelation**

The intellectual life of Nimāi Paṇḍit thus ended, demarcated by the birth of Caitanya Mahāprabhu, the Apostle of Kṛṣṇa-prema, The birth throes of Kṛṣṇa-prema in him were marked by what looked like abnormal moods of frenzy as of one possessed. He developed religious ecstasies and often behaved like one mad. He laughed, wept, incessantly shouted Kṛṣṇa's name, climbed up trees and raved in abstraction imagining himself to have caught hold of fleeing Kṛṣṇa or become united with him. He lost the notion of time, and sometimes thought that morning time was noon. The eight expressions of intense God-love — weeping, laughter, shivering, sweating, horripilation, fainting etc. — began to manifest in him. Profuse sweating was followed by dryness and heat in the body. Sometimes there were shivering, clenching and chattering of teeth. Again the body would become rigid like a piece of stone. Now the breathing would stop and next begin to blow like a gale. The body, now heavy, would next become so light that one could easily lift him in one's arm. At times the body would curve like a circle, or following a hiccup, his otherwise golden countenance would lose all colour. Often the colour of the eyes changed, and the hair stood on end, with plum-like pimples at their roots, oozing blood. These are explained in the genuine writings of contemporary chroniclers. Such external manifestations of the onset of Kṛṣṇa-prema were sometimes very uncontrollable and turbulent in nature. It was only sometime after that his mental feelings and attitudes became more coherent, disciplined and within his own control.

Many Paṇḍits of Nadia who were ill-disposed towards him could recognise in these development only abnormal manifestations and circulated the scandal that Nimāi Paṇḍit had become mad. But the few true devotees in that region perceived in them the surge of divine emotion, and some recognised in him a divine Incarnation. One of them was

Advaita Ācārya, a pious Vaiṣṇava of Śāntipur in the neighbourhood, accepted by many as the leader of the Vaiṣṇava community. When several Vaiṣṇavas went to him to report about the great transformation of Nimāi Paṇḍit, Advaita said that the previous night he had a dream in which Kṛṣṇa revealed to him the message. "Grieve no more. Your prayers have been heard. I myself am come to teach the way of salvation to men." When he opened his eyes he saw Nimāi standing before him.

Another person to recognise the real identity of Nimāi was the great devotee Śrīvas. There is a revealing incident connected with him. Many of the detractors of Nimāi had gone on a deputation to the Muslim ruler of Bengal, Hussain Shah,* and reported to him that there would be no peace in their part of the country unless he sent his police to arrest Nimāi and his Vaiṣṇava devotees performing their noisy Kīrtans. The Vaiṣṇavas were a little frightened on hearing this. It required a miracle of Nimāi to restore their confidence.

One of those days the devotee Śrīvas was performing worship in his home shrine. A knock was heard at his door, and to the annoyed enquiry he made, a voice replied, "I am He whom you are trying to commune with." On the door being opened, the bright figure of Nimāi went in to the utter surprise of Śrīvas and sat on the seat notionally kept empty for the Deity. To Śrīvas who was standing

* The Sena dynasty which was ruling Gauḍa (Bengal) began to decline from the time of ascension of Lakṣmaṇa Sena (1069). Social decline and political instability caused utter disruption of the life of the people. This facilitated the extension of Muslim aggression into Bengal under Baktiyār. This aggression was only an overflow of the Muslim invasion of India, which had begun much earlier and the Lhodi dynasty (1451-1526) was ruling at Delhi. It was only after Hussain Ṣhah ascended the throne of Gauḍa (Bengal) in 1493 that the country got a sōmewhat stable and well-administered Government. When Caitanya was a teen-ager, Hussain Shah was ruling over Bengal with his capital at Ramkeli (now in Maldah Dist.). So this complaint was lodged before his Governor (the Kāzi) who administered the areas around Navadvip.

Padmavasan

speechless, he gave the order, "Fetch water, I want to bathe." When he moved to the bath room, they saw a figure of gold lit as with "a million lightning flashes". The water flowing from his body seemed luminous. When he went back to the room of worship, people began to hear the entrancing sound of the flute. Devotees soon brought heaps of flowers, sandal paste and offerings. He then wanted to be taken to the bed room. Then he declared, "I am He who sits in the hearts of all men. I have revealed myself to tell you that you have nothing to fear from the Muslim King. This time I have come not to punish the sinners but to reclaim them. I have come to teach my creatures how to attain Me by Bhakti and Prema. I shall show you how I shall change the heart of the king." Then to demonstrate his power, he called a little girl who was standing by and said, "O Nārāyaṇī, be inspired by the love of Kṛṣṇa." Immediately she fell into an ecstasy. Nimāi then added, "This is how I shall deal with the king". A little later he said, "I am going. I shall come again in good time." With these words Nimāi lost external consciousness. When he came round, he himself wondered how he was there in the house of Śrīvas and he began to pray loudly like a devotee, "O merciful Kṛṣṇa! Save me from all worldly desires and draw me towards your lotus feet." Thus he revealed that there were two in him, Nimāi the devotee and Nimāi the Lord.

These incidents opened the eyes of several people of Nadia, especially of the Paṇḍits proud of their learning. They found that Bhakti was not mere vapid emotional nonsense, but something solid and substantial that can be given by a great Master to others at his will. This notion became still more confirmed when Nimāi demonstrated this power again by imparting Kṛṣṇa Bhakti to a neighbour and friend Gadādhar and a vainglorious ascetic Śuklāmbar, by blessing them with a touch of his hand.

## The Gathering of Some Important Followers

A few remarkable personages, who played an important part in Nimāi's later life, now began to gather round him. The first and foremost of those to gather was an ascetic named Nityānanda. There is an unconfirmed tradition that he was none other than Nimāi's elder brother Viśvarūp who had turned ascetic and wandered forth from home years back. Whatever be the truth about it, this Nityānanda had turned ascetic in early life, and after visiting many places, he went to Vṛndāvan, where he met Īśvar Purī. Purī advised him that if his object was to see Śrī Kṛṣṇa, he should go to Nadia. Nimāi had already the fore-knowledge that a great being, who was identical with Balaram, the brother of Kṛṣṇa, was coming to meet him. He gave out the name of the expected person as Nitāi. After some search in Nadia, he was found out. They both met as old friends, and on their meeting, Nitāi had a sudden vision of Gauraṇga with six arms. In the first two he held a bow and an arrow as Rāma, in the second pair he held a flute as Kṛṣṇa, and in the third pair a Daṇḍa (stick) and a Kamaṇḍalu (water pot) as a Sannyāsin. The vision threw him into a trance. The Master then touched him with the blessing. "Arise! All your wishes will be fulfilled. You shall carry with you the fountain of Bhakti and Prema." Thereafter Nitāi (shortened form of Nityānanda) always followed Nimāi like a shadow.

Another person to come close to him was Advaita Ācārya, a scholarly and wealthy leader of the Vaiṣṇavas, staying at Śāntipūr, ten miles away from Navadvip. Though Nimāi had, as already said, revealed his identity to him much earlier, it was only after crossing many hurdles of doubts and scepticism, that he would accept Nimāi's divinity.

Yet another important person to join him was Pauṇḍarika, a saintly person from Cittagong. But the most remarkable one was a Mulsim devotee named Haridās who took to the practice of loud and protracted singing of Hari's name. For becoming a Viṣṇava the Kāzi, the Muslim ruler's agent, condemned him to the Korānic punishment to be given to such an apostate. He was to be subjected to lashes in the different villages of the place until the man died. Like Prahlāda of the Bhāgavata no torture could kill him. As the lashes fell on him he felt only thrills of bliss, and he prayed that his ignorant tormenters might be pardoned by the Lord. After a time he fell into a trance creating a great upheaval of devotional fervour in the crowd that had gatherd around. The guards finally threw his unconscious body into the river, thinking him dead. Soon he revived with the touch of cool water and scrambled to the shore. The report of these incidents caused a conversion in the mind of the Kāzi too, who soon came to pay his respects to Haridās.

**Changing Moods of Nimāi**

In those days Nimāi's mood often used to change. From a devotee pining for God, Nimāi would all of a sudden manifest the glory and power of the Divinity attracting the worshipful reverence of all surrounding him. An example of this took place in the house of Śrīvās one day where a similar occurrence had already taken place earlier. In a Divine mood he seated himself in the seat of Viṣṇu, with devotees surrounding him. The room was lighted with the effulgence emanating from his body. A sweet smile and indescribable loveliness graced his face. People felt that they were face to face with the Lord of the Universe. They brought flowers in heaps. The large concourse of devotees did their worship without any hustling or commotion, each absorbed in the devotional mood and oblivious of others in that awesome presence. They all brought large quantities of food offerings which they pressed him to take. He took all that food enough to satisfy the hunger of a 'thousand men'. The Lord looked silent and serene. Each one felt that he was looking at him only. Soon it was nightfall and devotees thought of doing Ārati to the Lord. They fetched Śaci, Nimāi's mother, as the proper person to do this, telling her that he was, not her son but the Lord of all. The old lady then bowed down to him. The person who had till now treated Śaci as his mother, now planted his feet on her head. She immediately fell into a trance and began to dance. Though ignorant of Sānskrit, she began to chant from the Bhāgavata Purāṇa, the hymn addressed to Kṛṣṇa by His mother Devaki.

He now called some devotees one by one and addressed them. He called Śrīdhar, an insignificant man, who used to supply him plantain leaves, and blessed him. He fell into a trance. He offered to give to Śrīdhar even a kingdom if he asked for it, but Śrīdhar asked only to be privileged to be the servant of his devotees.

Then he called Murāri, a worshipper of Rāma and Sītā. Murāri saw him as Rāma accompanied by Sītā. He advised him, and through him Advaita Ācārya, to give up interest in occultism, as it would not help any one to attain God.

Next Haridās, the Muslim devotee, was summoned. He testified to the devotees that as the lashes cut into his flesh he felt no pain. Nimāi asked all whether any one wanted any boon, but all refused to have anything except Bhakti. But Mukunda, a devotee of angelic nature, was not summoned but neglected. The poor man was standing outside weeping. Śrīvās therefore asked the Lord why that devotee was thus neglected. The reply was that he would see him only after ten millions of births. When this was communicated to him, Mukunda began to dance in joy; for, the great devotee that he was, he did not mind waiting even for ten million births, if he could see the Lord after that. When the others pushed Mukunda to his presence, the Lord addressed the assembled devotees that his object in dealing with Mukunda in this way was to test faith and show others what true devotion and surrender meant.

This manifestation of the Lord as Almighty lasted till midnight and then this mood gave way to the All-sweet.

The Bhaktas felt that the ever-new beauty of the all-perfect Lord overflowed their eyes. He took the devotees one by one and embraced them all. The Bhaktas then experienced the true relation between Kṛṣṇa, Rādhā and the Gopis. Just as his power aspect was too much for the devotees to bear, so was his sweetness too. So they appealed to him to present himself as purely human as before and free them from the tension of his awesome Divine presence. "Yes", he said and then with a shriek he fell down. Thus ended what is called Mahā Prakāśa, the great Revelation. It took a long time for him to regain his normal consciousness. All signs of death appeared on his face; but when a song of Rādhā's attendants to their mistress was sung, his link with the normal human consciousness was gradually restored. Then the devotees all began to dance in joy, raising peals of the devotional slogan 'Hari-bol'

## Conversion of Jagāi and Mādhāi

Nimāi and his followers were holding their Hari-kīrtans mostly within closed doors at night and the devotees taking part were mostly drawn from lower castes. This gave ground for criticism of the sect by some sections, especially Brāhmaṇas who were proud of their learning and aristocratic traditions. Nimāi and his devotees now thought that they should not waste their day time but engage themselves in carrying the message of divine love (Kṛṣṇa-bhakti) from door to door. In contrast to the way of pure renunciation for overcoming sexuality, the seed of all sin and suffering, Bhakti was projected as the means for transforming it. Śiva, the lord of renunciation, burnt Cupid by an angry look, but Kṛṣṇa is Madana-mohana or one who could infatuate Cupid himself. So Nimāi and his followers decided to spread Kṛṣṇa-bhakti all over the place by going from door to door with Kṛṣṇa-kīrtans and exhortations to holy living. Large numbers of ordinary people responded to their call but the proud Brāhmaṇas did not and interpreted the visits of these Vaiṣṇavas as spying on behalf of thieves.

Nityānanda therefore suggested to Haridās that if they could convert Jagāi and Mādhāi, they would be able to make an impression on their detractors. Now these two, Jagai and Mādhāi nominally Kotvals or police officers of the place, were confirmed drunkards and rowdies. They were noted bullies and a terror to all people. When Nityānanda and Haridās first went to them with their message of Bhakti, they treated them with contempt and jocularly drove them away. Again they went with a big Kīrtan party with Caitanya in the centre. The noise annoyed the bullies who were having their siesta. Enraged, they threw big brickbats at Nityānanda and Haridās who were at the head of the party. Nityānanda began to bleed profusely, but still he continued to dance, singing the Lord's name. Now Nimāi himself approached the bullies and accosted them. The bullies felt a fierce and irresistible ball of fire was coming towards them. It is interpreted by biographers as Viṣṇu's weapon, the discus known as Sudarśana Cakra. Being stunned, as it were, the bullies stood trembling from head to feet. Nityānanda now interceded with the Lord on their behalf, requesting him not to destroy but save them. The Lord thereupon embraced Jagāi and Mādhāi. At that transforming touch the moral lepers were at once changed into saintly characters. The Lord had taken upon Himself the burden of all their sins. The erstwhile bullies were now writhing in the agony of repentence and wanted to ask forgiveness of all the residents of the place. For this they took their seat for days at the bathing ghat where most people gathered for bath, asking pardon of the people and requesting the crowds to trample on them as punishment for the wrongs they had done. In course of time by their personal labour they made a ghat on the river, which still exists and is called Mādhāi's ghat.

**The Kāzi's Transformation**

The conversion of Jagāi and Mādhāi made a tremendous impact on the people in general and led to a phenomenal increase in the number of Nimāi's followers. The streets of Nadia began to reverberate day and night with Hari-kīrtans. The attainment of such wide acceptance of Nimāi and his doctrine was not at all pleasing to the learned and aristocratic Brāhmaṇas of the place. Especially his discarding of caste considerations in spiritual matters was anathema to them. They felt that this would lead gradually to a total disappearance of their importance and influence in society.

So they conspired to complain again against Nimāi to the Kāzi, the local governor of the Muslim ruler of Bengal on the ground that the work of Nimāi and his followers was undermining the religion of the place and unless they were checked it would eventually lead to great social unrest affecting the stability of the State. To the Muslim, Brāhmaṇas and Vaiṣṇavas were all alike infidels, but the Kāzi felt it was his duty to intervene if it was going to affect the stability of the State. So he issued immediate orders to stop all Hari-kīrtans, but it had no effect. So he sent his police to arrest Nimāi and his followers, but they were unable to do so, as huge crowds surrounded them. This inflamed the Kāzi all the more and he let loose some of his Afghan troops to ruthlessly attack and disperse these rebellious people. But devotion had eliminated fear from the people's hearts. When they were attacked at one part of the city, they gathered at another, and thus the Kīrtan parties continued for some time, but eventually they were silenced.

Now the Lord himself took up the challenge. He issued a call to people to gather, and a huge crowd with the Lord in the centre leading them, went as a Kīrtan party in a mood of devotional frenzy to the house of the Kāzi. They wanted to interview the Kāzi. Though at first a little afraid to do so, he finally came out and was face to face with the Lord. The mood of the all-powerful governor immediately changed, and he began to talk in an attitude of humility. Addressing the Lord as Hari-gaur, the Kāzi said that he had taken action not because he wanted, but because the leaders of Hindu society had prompted him to do so. Further he said, "There is only one God; the Hindus call him Nārāyaṇa. People say you are He. Is it so?" The Lord then held one finger of the Kāzi and said, "You have uttered the holy names of Hari, Kīrtan and Nārāyaṇa. So all your sins are forgiven." The Kāzi was at once transformed. Tears gushed out of his eyes, and he prostrated himself before the Lord in humble submission. Immediately he promulgated an order that none should interfere with the Kīrtans.

**Advaita Ācārya**

Another hostile element that the Lord converted into his religion of Bhakti was Advaita Ācārya. Though the Ācārya had many occasions to see the divinity of Nimāi, still he was unconvinced and was of the view that what Nimāi felt were subjective hallucinations. Though respected by the Vaiṣṇavas as a leader, he did not believe in the emotional Bhakti that Nimāi was propagating. He believed in Knowledge (Jñāṇa) as the ultimate discipline and devotion (Bhakti) as the way of life for inferior people. Nimāi wanted to change his attitude completely. So with this in view, he went one day to Advaita's home at Śāntipūr, which was about twelve miles away from Navadvip. In an exalted mood, he asked Advaita why he was teaching the wrong theory that Jñāna is superior to Bhakti. When Advaita refused to answer, he rained blows on him with a stick. Though others there protested against the conduct of Nimāi, Advaita himself was enjoying the beating. Beaming with delight, he exclaimed, "I forsook Him, and He has come here all the way to win me back. Who has more mercy than my merciful Lord?" A little while after, the Lord said loudly, "If you should resort to Jñāna for salvation, you had no business to pray for an Avatār." This was to remind Advaita that he had manifested himself on earth in response to Advaita's prayer to turn the people's mind to the right path. This announcement was a surprise to the Ācārya. The Lord has many ways of infusing Bhakti. In regard to some he did it with a look, with others by a touch and with still others by a blessing. But in Advaita's case he adopted a radical step.

## Transformation into Rādhā's Mood

The savants of the Vaiṣṇava school maintain that Caitanya was Rādhā and Kṛṣṇa come in one body. In His Vṛndāvana episode Rādhā tasted the Bliss that was Kṛṣṇa in various forms of love. Kṛṣṇa now felt that He should enjoy His own Bliss as Rādhā did. It was to fulfil this that in the Caitanya incarnation, He was Rādhā and Kṛṣṇa combined in one personality. He could therefore be Kṛṣṇa in one mood and Rādhā in another. Till now Kṛṣṇa, the granter of Bhakti and the protector of all, was more manifest in him. Now when he was about twentyfour, the Rādhā-mood began to possess him more. He had taught Bhakti till then and now he wanted to teach Prema (intense love) by his own example. Rādhā's intense and intimate love of Kṛṣṇa as a paramour in separation and in union had to be illustrated by his own example. This is said to be the significance of the awakening of the Rādhā mood in him. Earlier to his advent the great composer and poet Jayadeva had described it in all detail in his great composition Gītā-govinda, which had already become very popular. But in Caitanya's after-life, this aspect of divine love, designated as Prema in contrast to Bhakti, was demonstrated as an actual fact.

This change in mood was signalled by the recurrence of frequent mental upheavals and psychic disturbances, as when he returned from Gaya after initiation by Īśvar Purī. These had partially subsided and he had reestablished control over such states. Now with the growth of the Rādhā mood he began to heave sighs of longing, and manifest agonising pangs of separation and swooning.

Besides, he began to express his desire to leave Navadvip and go to Vṛndāvan where alone Kṛṣṇa could be met. This meant abandoning hearth and home, mother and wife, friends, and devotees, to become a Sannyāsin as his elder brother Viśvarūp had done. There was also the feeling in him that so long as he remained as Nimāi Paṇḍit with close relatives and assets of his own, his critics, the sophisticated Brāhmaṇa Paṇḍits of Nadia, would not feel convinced of the new doctrine he preached, and thus his mission in life could not be fulfilled unless he became a Sannyāsin.

When the devotees got scent of this, they tried their best to deter him from his resolution. But the greatest hurdle on the way were his mother Śaci and his wife Viṣṇupriyā. After much persuasion and subtle appeals he got their extremely unwilling consent. And one night in January 1510, without the knowledge of any one, when the whole of Navadvip was asleep, he stole away from home, crossed the river by swimming and ran towards Katva, sixteen miles away, lest any one pursuing him should overtake him.

## Adopting Sannyāsa

At Katva lived Keśav Bhārati with whom Nimāi had some contact in early days. He now went to him to beseech him to admit him into the Order of Sannyāsins. But he had to face several difficulties before he could get this end accomplished. A search party headed by Nityānanda had gone to Katva, suspecting that Nimāi might have gone to meet some Sannyāsin. Keśav Bhārati himself was non-plussed as to what he should do. A handsome young man brought up in affluent circumstances, with an aged mother and a young wife at home — to take to Sannyāsa which meant a life of wandering and subsistence on what chance might bring! Seeing the magnificent personality of Nimāi shining like gold, a crowd gathered. But Nimāi was not aware of all the surroundings. His mind was absorbed in Rādhā's sentiment of separation from Kṛṣṇa and her poignant anxiety to see Him. He must go to Vṛndāvan for this, abandoning all the fetters of the world. The soul in the state of Samsāra is wedded to the body. Renunciation for the Vaiṣṇava meant the breaking of this wedlock and getting wedded to the Lord.

Keśav Bhārati at first refused to give him Sannyāsa, first because by virtue of Kṛṣṇa Prema Nimāi was already greater than himself, and next he had not received the willing and full permission of his old mother and youthful wife to abandon them and take to the life of asceticism. The devotees from Nadia and the local citizens of status and learning all joined in this effort to block Nimāi's decision. But nothing would deter Nimāi. The one thought of going to Vṛndāvan and meeting Kṛṣṇa after abandoning all worldly fetters made him oblivious of every other idea or even of the devotees surrounding him. By very clever persuasion and the intensity of his spirit of renunciation, he was able to overcome the unwillingness of Keśav Bhārati. The ascetic at last initiated him into Sannyāsa and gave him the name of Kṛṣṇa Caitanya — one who evoked the consciousness of Kṛṣṇa in the minds of men.

Soon Kṛṣṇa Caitanya started westward, goaded by his mad longing to reach Vṛndāvan and meet Kṛṣṇa. For five days he walked without food or rest through fields and forests in the region known as Rārḥ until he lost his way and began to enquire of stray passers by about the way to Vṛndāvan. Nityānanda, who was pursuing him, had gone in advance, and meeting a batch of cowboys in a region that Caitanya would be passing through, taught them to sing Hari-bol, and also instructed them to misdirect Caitanya to the way towards the Gaṅgā as the road to Vṛndavana. This would lead the new ascetic to Śāntipur, the residence of Advaita Ācārya. The strategem clicked and soon Caitanya found himself at Śāntipur when his normal consciousness dawned on him.

Devotees now gathered round, and when the news spread to Navadvip, streams of people began to treck from there to Śāntipur to see their familiar Nimāi Paṇḍit as the Sannyāsin Śrī Kṛṣṇa Caitanya. Cries of Hari-bol and ecstatic dancing went on continuously at Śāntipur. Even the proud intellectuals of Nadia were converted by the force of renunciation he exemplified. Nityānanda now brought Śaci, the mother of Nimāi, too along with others. The meeting between the mother and the lost son presented a very piquant scene. She was also taken up with the festive mood that prevailed, and insisted on herself cooking for her son in the feasts that were arranged during the ten days of Caitanya's stay at Advaita's house. Under the compelling sense of his obligation towards his mother, Caitanya communicated through devotees that he was even prepared to return to Nadia if she insisted. But the high-minded lady that she was, her regard for her son's reputation as a Sannyāsin prevailed over the pursuit of her own self-interest. So she gave her full consent to her son's departure from home as a Sannyāsin, with the caveat that in place of Vṛndāvan he might go to Nīlācal (Jagannāth Puri). The former place was far off, more than two thousand miles away, whereas Nīlācal was close by and she could get news of him frequently and he could even visit Bengal occasionally. Once this agreement was arrived at, Caitanya immediately rose up with a 'Hari-bol' and began to walk rapidly to Nīlācal accompanied by a few of his intimate devotees — Nityānanda, Mukunda, Jagadānanda, Govinda, Dāmodar and Haridās.

**Trip to Jagannāth Puri**

The yearning to meet Kṛṣṇa, at Vṛndāvan now got transformed and seized him with the same intensity to meet Puruṣottama of Nīlācal, who is none other than Kṛṣṇa himself. With little food and rest he practically ran most of the distance and passed through the region now known as Calcutta, a jungle at that time, and soon reached the border between Bengal and Orissa or Kaliṅga as it was then known. As there was hostility between the rulers of the two countries, no one was allowed to cross the border by the guards stationed there. The personality of the young ascetic however won over the commander of the border forces and he was permitted to go his way.

He halted at Remuna, some six miles north west of Bālesvar in Orissa, at the temple of Gopīnāth, about whose Kher Prasād he had heard much from Īśvar Purī. Īśvar Purī's preceptor Mādhav Purī had once wandered some two thousand miles from Vṛndāvan to this place and had several miraculous experiences there. Mādhav Purī had installed the image of Gopāla as Govardhana-dhārī (uplifter of Govardhana) on a hill near Vṛndāvan and made arrangements for regular worship. But Govardhana-dhārī commanded Purī in a dream that he should go to Nīlācal and get sandalwood from there and rub him with its paste to cool his body. So the devout Mādhav Purī went all the way braving all perils, and at Remuna he halted at the temple of Gopīnāth. He sang and danced in ecstasy before the beautiful image. On enquiring about the Bhog offered to the deity, he learnt that twelve pots of Amṛt Keli or Cream of Nectar made by condensing milk, which was unrivalled in taste, were offered everyday. Purī desired to taste it, but would not beg for it. Mysteriously the Lord himself commanded the priest to give a pot of it to Purī. Then Mādhav Purī went to Nīlācal and with the help of the ruler's agent got one maund of sandal wood and twenty tolas of camphor. With this he started his return journey, and on the way stopped at the temple of Gopīnāth again. There he had a dream in which Govardhana-dhārī, whom he had installed earlier at Vṛndāvan, appeared to him and told him that he need not carry all that sandal wood to Vṛndāvan passing through perilous countries ruled by Muslims. It was enough if he applied it over the image of Gopāl at Remuna itself, as Gopal and himself (Govardhana-dhārī) were the same. The Lord had put Purī to all this tribulation only to test his faith. Gaurānga narrated the whole story of Mādhav Purī to his followers in detail and then recited a verse composed by Purī at the last moment of his life conveying his identification with Rādhā's love for Kṛṣṇa. It runs. "O Lord! gracious to the lowly! Thou art now in Mathura. When will Thou come to me? Darling mine! My heart runs about in pain of longing to see Thee. What shall I do?"

Reciting this verse, the Master dropped down in ecstasy with intensity of love. Lifted up by Nityānanda, he ran hither and thither in a transport of devotion, shouting, laughing, dancing and singing. His voice was choked with emotion and tears were running down his cheeks. He trembled, perspired, wept in joy, stood still, changed colour — now showing remorse, now grief, now stupor, now pride, exaltation or meekness. He passed that night at the temple of Gopīnāth singing and dancing. The priests presented him and his followers with four pots of their famous Amṛt Keli.

**Worship of Sākṣi Gopāl**

Next he halted at Jaipur and worshipped at the shrine of Varāha with ecstatic singing and dancing. At Katak he went to worship at the temple of Sākṣi Gopal. The beauty of the image threw him into ecstasy. There, Nityānanda who had visited this temple in earlier days, narrated the legends connected with the naming of the Deity as Sākṣi or witness. According to the legend, in order to save a devotee from an awkward situation, the image walked with the devotee all the way from Vṛndāvan on the understanding that the devotee would not look back in the course of his travel. When he reached his village situated nearly forty mile from Katak, the devotee looked back to see if the Deity was actually coming with him. The image therefore stopped there to bear witness to the truth of His devotee's claim. The image can still be seen at the place.

## Arrival at Puri and Meeting Sārvabhauma

Then passing through Bhuvanesvar, the Master reached the river Bhāgri, six miles away from Puri, from where the temple tower could be seen. He felt that Kṛṣṇa was beckoning him from the top of the temple and immediately fell into an ecstasy. He moved slowly, dancing, shouting and laughing, thus making a thousand leagues of those six miles.

## Arrival at Puri & Conversion of Sārvabhauma

Reaching the temple premises, Caitanya insisted on going within alone, even though he was warned by his followers that the image of the Deity was fully guarded by temple servants, and none would be allowed to approach him. Breaking the line of the guards in the temple, he rushed like one frenzied towards the image to embrace Jagannāth and in the process fell down. The angry guards were about to assault him when they were stopped by a tall and venerable Brāhmaṇa who was, as it were, sent by Providence to protect the devotee. That personage was none other than Pandit Vāsudeva Sārvabhauma, the doyen of scholars of the time, who had come from Navadvip and settled at Puri at the invitation of King Pratāparudra who ruled over Orissa at that time. Caitanya himself was, as Nimai, a student of Sārvabhauma's in his Navadvip days. The great Paṇḍit felt a strange attraction to the young Sannyāsin and had him transported to his house by his students. The very touch of the young Sannyāsin roused a wave of devotional fervour in them, making them all shout 'Hari-bol' and dance in ecstasy. This impressed Sārvabhauma, who, though a scholar and a follower of all the orthodox customs, was not at heart a Bhakta, a devotee. Still at this moment the devotional sentiment got a temporary hold on him and he touched the feet of Caitanya.

His pride of scholarship however soon asserted itself and made him question his conclusion. For, his estimate of the Sannyāsin had been made without sufficient proof. He, however, extended hospitality and provided accommodation for Caitanya and the devotees. He now adopted a patronising attitude towards Caitanya, and advised him that he was too young to be an ascetic, that his devotional fervour, singing, dancing etc., were mere eccentricities and aberrations, and that he should now learn Vedānta under him and turn a new leaf in his life. The Master accepted the proposal in all humility. So one day the Paṇḍit read some Vedāntic passages with Śaṅkara's commentary and gave a very scholarly explanation. After a time he asked the young ascetic whether he was following his exposition, and got the shocking reply that the Vedāntic text was in itself simple enough for him to understand, but as for Śaṅkara's commentary and its elucidation, he could not understand even a word, as it all looked like absurdity to him.

This direct challenge to his scholarship came as a great blow to the Paṇḍit who considered himself invincible in debate. Then for a verse from the Bhāgavata for which the Paṇḍit gave nine meanings, Caitanya supplied many more, after showing fallacies in the Paṇḍit's interpretation. Though proud of his scholarship, the Paṇḍit had an open mind, and the clarity and cogency of the young Sannyāsin's words made him convinced that he needed no instruction. He declared that he was Vedamaya (full of Vedic wisdom), and the Vedas were only like a plaything to him. The Master now replied that the Vedas taught only Prema and Bhakti and not the conclusions of soulless logic and pedantry.

Defeated in his own familiar field of scholarship, Sārvabhauma surrendered himself to Caitanya and prostrated at his feet. When he got up and looked, what he saw was not the young ascetic. In his place stood a six-armed divinity. In two of his hands he carried a bow and arrows, with two others he played on a flute, and in the remaining two he carried a mendicant's staff and bowl. The sight put

Sārvabhauma into a state of rapt Samādhi. When the Samādhi was over, Sārvabhauma found only the young mendicant in place of that Divine figure. The scholar understood from this that He who appeared as Rāma and Kṛṣṇa had now incarnated as a mendicant. Still there persisted in his mind the doubt that what he experienced might be a hallucination.

Next day very early in the morning, the Master, after having worshipped in the temple, came with some offered food stuff and knocked at Sārvabhauma's door even before he had got up. He sat with the Paṇḍit and asked him to take some of the food offerings. It was against the rigid customs of the Brāhmaṇas to take food before a bath and Sandhyā-vandanam in the morning. At the command of the Master, the Paṇḍit was ready to violate even the most sacred established customs for the sake of God. The law of Prema-bhakti is as Rādhā had sung: "Listen! The flute of my Beloved is beckoning me. I must go. If you are afraid of what others would say, do not come near me. My beloved cannot be won without sacrifice. If you desire to capture Him, you must first surrender everything to Him."

Sārvabhauma had now performed this surrender. He had now thrown away his adherence to ceremonial piety. The Lord embraced him, and immediately, he fell into ecstasy. Coming back to body consciousness, he began to dance inebriated with the bliss of Bhakti and the name of Hari on his lips. His pride of scholarship was now completely dissipated. Prostrating before the Lord, he recited in praise of Him a hundred verses that he composed extempore. He recognised that though Caitanya looked like a man, he was divine. The fabled philosopher's stone may look like an ordinary stone, but if it touches a hard piece of iron, the iron becomes gold. A confirmed logician, more tough and hard than a piece of iron, now became soaked with the soft sentiment of Bhakti by Caitanya's touch. The six-handed divine figure (perhaps a replica of it) that

Sārvabhauma saw can still be seen installed in the temple of Puri. Sārvabhauma's conversion meant the conversion of the whole scholarly world of Puri to Caitanya's devotional cult. Eventually even Pratāpa Rudra, the Ruler of Kalinga and patron of Sārvabhauma, came to recognise Caitanya's greatness, and often visited him to pay his obeisance. Gradually the flood of Caitanya's Prema-Bhakti covered the whole of Orissa which began to resound with Kṛṣṇa-Kīrtan.

**Pilgrimage to the South**

Caitanya's stay at Puri on this first visit was very short — according to some a fortnight and according to others four months. He now expressed his resolution to go alone to Southern regions on pilgrimage, ostensibly to discover his elder brother Visvarūpa but really to spread the religion of love in these regions. The pilgrimage took two full years starting from 10th April 1510. All his Navadvip devotees like Nityānanda and the new ones like Sārvabhauma were very sad, but when he had resolved one way, the soft-hearted Caitanya was like adamant. With Kṛṣṇadāsa as his sole companion, he started with his waterpot and loin cloth alone as his property. Sārvabhauma requested him to meet in the course of his journey Rāmānanda Roy, who was the Kalinga King Gajapati Pratāpa Rudra's Governor at Vidyānagar on the bank of the Godāvari. He was told that though not a Brāhmaṇa Paṇḍit, Caitanya would find in him an extraordinary type of devotee.

Caitanya travelled along the east coast to the south upto Setubandha and Kanyākumāri, and then turned back to Puri travelling through Central India, Western India and Ganges valley. Besides the numerous villages through which he passed, he halted for varying periods at fiftytwo important holy places according to the chronicles of his itenary kept by Kṛṣṇa Dāsa who accompanied him. Everywhere his personality attracted large crowds and he inspired them by his chanting of Kṛṣṇa's name and ecstatic dance. He manifested in these travels the magnetic power of his devotional fervour much more than he did at Nadia. In some places he made a whole village, irrespective of people's caste or creed, dance with chanting of Kṛṣṇa's name and turned them into true Vaiṣṇavas. In important centres of learning and in headquarters of religious sects, he met the theological authorities and generated in them respect for his religion of pure love centering on Rādhākṛṣṇa, in which caste distinctions had no place, which discounted the need of scholarship and logic chopping, and which attached little importance to meticulous ceremonials and ritualism. Only a few important occurrences can be described here.

**Meeting with Rāmānanda Roy**

The most noted event in this pilgrimage was his meeting with Rāmānanda Roy at Vidyānagar, as suggested by Vāsudeva Sārvabhauma. Vidyānagar, (not to be confused with Vijayanagar) was a place situated to the east of modern Rājahmundry at a strategic point. Rāmānanda Roy was the Governor of that place. Caitanya met Governor Roy at the bathing ghat of the holy Godāvari, while he was resting after a bath. The sight of Caitanya's spiritual lustre attracted Roy to that visiting Sannyāsin. He went near him and made humble obeisance. Soon they entered into conversation, which resulted in each admiring the other for the wisdom and devotion they both revealed. Recognising the divinity of Caitanya, Roy requested him to stay at Vidyānagar at least for ten days. Caitanya complied with the request.

In the course of the conversation they had during the nights, Caitanya, continuously interrogating Roy, revealed the subtlest teachings regarding devotion to Kṛṣṇa, making Roy his instrument. From the earliest stages of the growth of devotional sentiment, Roy was made to traverse the whole gamut of Bhakti ending with the love of Rādhā and her Sakhis (comrades) for Kṛṣṇa without the least trace of selfishness. First Caitanya asked him what the means of gaining devotion was. Roy answered that performance of one's duties as offering to God was the means. He was asked to go deeper. Roy answered that abandoning all one's caste duties for the love of God and taking refuge in Him alone were the means. Commanded to go still deeper, Roy gave answers revealing step after step the profundities of love for Kṛṣṇa. Devotion mixed with knowledge of God's Mahātmya, or divine majesty, was discounted. For, this would jeopardise pure love with an element of awe. Besides to know is to analyse, but to love is to be attracted. He is the soul of our soul and love must be a sense of intimacy. Roy next mentioned fraternal love, love as Balaram had for Kṛṣṇa, as a still deeper form of love. Asked to go still deeper, Roy mentioned parental love like what Nanda and Yaśodā had towards Child Kṛṣṇa as a step still deeper. Being asked to say if there was still deeper form of love,Roy answered that it consisted in conjugal love — of the type Rukmiṇī and the wives of Kṛṣṇa had for him. The Lord was not satisfied even with this. So Roy mentioned that the illicit love that the Gopis had for Kṛṣṇa was still deeper. For, in such love a woman goes after her paramour without any consideration of his worth or of any social criticism or of any claim on him. She abandons herself to him. So should a devotee abandon himself to Kṛṣṇa. Asked to search his heart for any still deeper form of love, he answered Rādhā's love for Kṛṣṇa was the highest. For, that love was without the least taint of selfishness. Kṛṣṇa's propitiation was the only thing she cared for, and in pursuit of it no social persecution or personal sufferings would in the least deter her. She had sung: "Remind him of it, if he has forgotton it. At first we saw each other and the result was swift love. I do not know where it will lead me; for it is still growing. People say men and women fall in love with each other. But my condition was different. For I had no consciousness that he was a man and I am a woman. I cannot therefore account for my love of Kṛṣṇa.".

**Theology of Kṛṣṇa and Rādhā**

Pressed by the Master to reveal the whole mystery of Kṛṣṇa theology, Roy replied to the following effect: Kṛṣṇa is the Supreme Being, the source of all Incarnations, the First cause. He has His external Abode where he is eternally present. His body is pure Sat (Existence) Cit (Consciousness) and Ānanda (Bliss). At Vṛndāvan He appeared as the supernatural youthful Cupid (Manmatha), at whose adoration the formula recited is Love, the offering presented is the Seed of Love. There he drew all hearts — of men and women, of the animals and inanimate beings. He was Cupid's self, the conqueror of hearts (Bh.10.32.2). His own beauty charmed His own heart and He wished to embrace Himself. Such is Kṛṣṇa's Form

Now about Rādhā. Kṛṣṇa's powers are infinite, but three of them are the most important. These are Cit-śakti, Māyā-śakti and Jīva-śakti. The first is His internal and intrinsic Power (Svarupa-śakti); the second, His external creative Power (Māyā-śakti); and the third, His preservative or marginal Power (Jīva-śakti). Kṛṣṇa's Svarūpa-śakti has three kinds of manifestations according to the three aspects of Sat, Cit and Ānanda. Its Ānanda aspect is Hlādinī which gives bliss; It's Sat aspect is Sandhinī which is creative; and its Cit aspect is Saṁvit which is Jīva nature. What delights Kṛṣṇa is named Hlādinī. Kṛṣṇa is Himself delight and yet enjoys delight. Hlādinī is also what gives delight to the devotees, and the essence of Hlādinī is called Prema (Love). Prema is a series of emotions and the supreme form of it is known as Mahābhāva. Rādhā is the personification of this Mahābhāva, the highest expression of Hlādinī-śakti.

### The Conception of Sakhīs

The play of Rādhā and Kṛṣṇa is extremely deep. Moods like Dāsya (servitude), Vātsalya (paternal affection) etc., cannot comprehend it. The Sakhīs or the female associates of Rādhā alone can comprehend it. Those who adore Kṛṣṇa in the spirit of a Sakhī can alone enjoy this play to the fullness of its development. Votaries have therefore to practise devotion by adapting the attitude of these Sakhīs attending on Rādhā and Kṛṣṇa in their amorous dalliances.

The character of the Sakhīs defies all description. A Sakhī does not long to play with Kṛṣṇa all by herself. She feels a keener delight in contriving Kṛṣṇa's dalliance with Rādḥā. Rādhā is verily the wish-yielding creeper (Kalpalatā) of the love of Kṛṣṇa, and the Sakhīs are the leaves, flowers and shoots of the creeper. The nectar of dalliance of Rādhā with Kṛṣṇa waters this creeper, yielding to the Sakhīs forming its leaves and flowers delight ten million times more than if they themselves have been watered. The unselfish devotion of these towards each other strengthens the deliciousness (Rasa), and the sight of such unselfish love delights Kṛṣṇa.

The love felt by the Gopis is not lust (Kāma) at all. It is called Kāma for the sake of analogy, that being the only way in which it could be humanly expressed. Kāma or sexual lust cares only for sensual gratification for oneself. The Gopis on the other hand seek Kṛṣṇa's enjoyment, not theirs.

He whose heart is moved by the nectar of Gopi's passion, adores Kṛṣṇa, abandoning Vedic worship. By following the path of passionate love (Rāga) like the people of Vraja contemporaneous with Kṛṣṇa, one is born next in Vraja in the form of the person whose passion he imitated and thus gains Kṛṣṇa. By daily meditation on Kṛṣṇa's dalliance with Rādhā we are born as Sakhīs. You cannot attain Kṛṣṇa however much you adore Him as a Divinity. You attain Him by serving Him as a Gopī, as a Sakhī. In the ethereal body we meditate imitatively on the service rendered to Kṛṣṇa by a Sakhī and in the next birth we attain Rādhā-Krsna's feet as a Sakhī.

### Caitanya as Rādhā and Kṛṣṇa in One Personality

In this way talking on Rādhā-Kṛṣṇa and the spiritual love that they manifested, and singing and dancing, they spent the nights for ten days. At the end the Master manifested to Rāmānanda his real form. The Sannyāsin disappeared from view and in his place Rāmānanda found a form in which were blended Kṛṣṇa the Prince of Delight (Rasa) and Rādhā the Supreme Passive Enjoyment. Roy understood that in Caitanya incarnation Kṛṣṇa has taken on Himself the emotion and beauty of Rādhikā in order to taste His own delight. At the sight of this form Roy went into ecstasy. The Master touched him and brought him to normal consciousness, and confirming this understanding of his real nature told him: "I have shown you this form. My body is not of a fair complexion. But its present golden complexion is due to the contact with Rādhā's body. She touches none except the Prince of the Cowherds. I make my own heart imagine her emotions and thus I taste the delicious sweetness of Kṛṣṇa. Keep this matter a secret from the public." When after ten days the Master was about to depart he ordered Roy: "Give up your earthly concerns and go to Puri where I shall soon return after finishing my pilgrimage. There we shall live together passing our time happily in talking about Kṛṣṇa"

**Some Important Events in Other Places**

Caitanya's pilgrimage lasted for full two years. In his onward journey he touched all the important pilgrimage centres upto Setubandha and Kanyākumāri, moving quickly from place to place with the exception of certain important centres where he stayed for longer periods. One such place was Śrīraṅgam where he stayed with a pious person named Venkata Bhatta for the four months of Cāturmāsya. Every day he bathed in the Kāveri and sang and danced before Raṅganātha. It was there that he met a Brāhmaṇa who read the Gītā every day before the Deity without understanding its meaning in the least. Some scholars there used to scoff and hurl insulting words at this man, but he used to read with rapt attention in spite of the derision of these scholars. Seeing his tears of joy and tremor of body, the Master asked him what it was that inspired him and put him into rapture. He replied, "I am an ignorant man who does not understand the meaning of the words of the Gītā. Still I am reading it at the bidding of my Guru. When I do so my heart is rapt, beholding before my mind's eye the dark beauty of Kṛṣṇa as He sits on the chariot of Arjuna as its driver and gives His talk". To him the Master replied: "You alone are worthy to read the Gītā, and you alone understand its essence."

Venkata Bhatta with whom he stayed was devoted to Lakṣmī Nārāyaṇa. He belonged to Śrī-Vaiṣṇava sect which recognised Nārāyaṇa as the Deity. Through numerous remarks and scriptural quotations, Caitanya made him understand that Kṛṣṇa is the Deity and Nārāyaṇa is His emanation. He said, "Such is the sweetness of Kṛṣṇa that he wins the hearts of all. The people of Vṛndāvan knew Him not as God but as one among themselves. They knew Him as the son of the chief of Vraja and not as Godhead. Only those who adore Him in the manner of the people of Vṛndāvan can attain to Him. Nārāyaṇa and Kṛṣṇa are however one in essence. So are Lakṣmī and the Gopis. Lakṣmī in the garb of the Gopis tasted Kṛṣṇa's company. The devotional doctrine, however, does not recognise any plurality in Godhead. Devotees meditate on Him giving him different images." The Śrī-Vaiṣṇava Venkata Bhatta was thus persuaded to practise devotion to Kṛṣṇa.

At Madurai he stayed with a devotee Rāmadās who was practising fast in sorrow for the account given in Rāmāyaṇa that Rāvaṇa, a Rākṣasa, had touched the Divine Sītā and carried her away. The Master assured him that this was not correct. When he reached Setubandha he heard from the reading of the Kūrma Purāṇa that before Rāvaṇa came, Sītā had been given to the care of the Fire Deity and an illusory Sītā put in her place, that it was this Sītā that Rāvaṇa carried, and the fire ordeal of Sītā after Rāvaṇa's destruction was staged only to take back the original Sītā. Caitanya copied the page from the Purāṇa and on his return when he touched Madurai, he gave that copy to Rāmadās to assuage his grief.

On his return from Kanyākumāri he passed through the erstwhile Travancore State. There at Adi-keśava temple at Tiruvattar he found the rare manuscript of a Text called Brahma Samhitā, which is the cream of Vaiṣṇava scriptures, wherein all their dogmas and practices are given in a few words. He made a copy of it and carried it with him as a precious possession.

He went northward and visited Uḍupi the seat of Madhvācārya's religion. There the Tattva-Vādis, as the followers of that cult called themselves, at first looked down upon him as a Sannyāsin and a Māyāvādi. But seeing his devotional fervour and ecstasy at their Kṛṣṇa temple, they changed their view. To humble their pride the Master like an ignorant enquirer asked the high-priest of the Tattva-vādis what were the means to be adopted and the end to be sought by a devotee of Kṛṣṇa. The high priest gave the answer that the 'means' consisted in performing all duties as offering to Kṛṣṇa and the 'end' was the attainment of Vaikuṇṭha. Caitanya contradicted him with a scriptual quotation that a true Vaiṣṇava abjures both work and salvation. He abjures the fivefold salvation in Vaikuṇṭha, and seeks the service of Kṛṣṇa as his sole end. The High Priest could not contradict him, as this was the true Vaiṣṇava ideal.

He then passed through western and middle regions of India. In the land of the Gonds, the tribal chieftain Naoroji threatened to attack him unless he paid a ransom. Caitanya by an act of will converted him into a devotee. Not only did Naoroji give up his evil ways, but became an ascetic and a constant attendant of Caitanya.

He visited the famous Maharashtrian pilgrim centre of Paṇḍarīpuram and danced before Vittal and embraced the image. It is said in those regions he met the great saint Tukārām and imparted Kṛṣṇa-bhakti to him. At Paṇḍarīpuram he also met Śrīraṅga Purī, who like his own Guru Īśvar Purī was a disciple of Mādhavendra Purī who had visited Navadvip and stayed as a guest of his father. He also came to know that his elder brother Viśveśvar met with his end at Paṇḍarīpuram.

Among other important places where he halted in western India, Dvārakā was one. It was during his travels in these regions that he came across the great Text Kṛṣṇa-karṇāmṛta, a copy of which he carried as a precious possession. Then he travelled towards Puri passing through many holy places along the banks of Taptī, Narmadā and Godāvarī until he reached Vidyānagar, the place of his great devotee and friend Rāmānanda Roy.

**Return to Puri**

Advising Rāmānanda Roy again to resign his Governorship and inviting him to Puri, he reached that final destination of his after two years of pilgrimage and preaching of devotion for Kṛṣṇa. He was warmly received and adored by Vāsudeva Sārvabhauma to whom he confided two glad tidings, one, that the greatest devotee he met was Rāmānanda Roy, and the second, that the most precious possessions he got were Brahma Samhitā and Kṛṣṇa karṇāmṛta, which are unrivalled Gospels of Kṛṣṇa devotion. He popularised these Texts through his devotees and scholars of Orissa and Bengal.

The return of Caitanya was a matter of great rejoicing to the people of Puri. Kāśi Miśra vacated his house where the Master was accommodated. Sārvabhauma introduced to him all the servitors of the temple of Jagannāth as also all the important citizens of the place. Among those who sought permission to see the Master, one was Pratāpa Rudra, the King of Orissa himself. Though the king was a great devotee, Caitanya refused to meet him, as he, a

Ṣannyāsin, should not have anything to do with men of worldly position and importance, But Sārvabhauma and others contrived to bring the king in the garb of an ordinary devotee before the Master while he was singing and dancing along with devotees before the procession of Jagannāth on a car festival day. While the Master was in a trance King Pratāpa Rudra prostrated himself before him holding his feet. The king chanted melodiously verses from the Bhāgavata which had a soul-stirring effect on Caitanya who embraced him in a high spiritual mood and thereby transmitted Kṛṣṇa-bhakti to him.

The return of Caitanya to Nīlāchal created great expectations in the minds of the devotees at Navadvip. Batches of them, numbering all together about two hundred, came to meet him and stayed at Puri for about four months, during which time they enjoyed the hospitality of the temple authorities of Puri as arranged by Sārvabhauma. On every day the Master sang and danced in ecstasy with them. He divided them into four parties with himself in the middle. Eight Dholės (drums) and thirty two cymbals played on along with shouts of Hari reverberating the quarters. A flood of devotion bathed the whole of Puri with its waves of Hari's name. The Master then began to go round the temple followed by the four Kirtan parties. Often he fell down in ecstasy and had to be supported by Rāmānanda before he dashed on the ground. Thus he passed his time blissfully in ceaseless Saṅkīrtan with his followers.

**Car Festival**

When the Car Festival of the temple approached, he engaged himself and all his followers in cleaning that edifice, for which he was provided with a hundred water pots and brooms. Amidst the loud chant of Kṛṣṇa's name was performed the dusting, scrubbing and washing of the whole temple including its different shrines. Soon the day of the Car Festival came, and Jagannāth, after fifteen days of seclusion, came out in His gold embellished car as high as Sumeru mountain with an embroided canopy and fluttering banners around. Hundreds of fly whiskers and polished mirrors were hanging on the sides of the car. With every movement numerous mini-bells produced musical notes. The Master divided his party into seven, four preceding the car, two on both sides and one behind. It is said that the Master was miraculously seen in all the seven divisions simultaneously. He danced with all his might, manifesting in himself all the eight spiritual phases (Sāttvika Bhāvas) at the same time. His hair stood on end, with their roots in the skin bulging out; his teeth clashed together; blood oozed with the sweat flowing down his body; his lips uttered incoherent syllables; his tears moistened others as if they were being syringed; his complexion frequently changed, becoming at times rosy, at others like Mallika flower; he stood sometimes inert like dry wood and at others rolled on the ground breathing faintly and with froth coming out of his mouth. The car moved slowly amidst the vast crowds enthused by the devotional frenzy emanating from the son of Śaci. When it reached the garden of Balgandi, it stopped as it was time for offering noon Bhog to Jagannāth. Huge quantities of various kinds of food were heaped on all sides of the Deity in the car. The Master now withdrew to the verandah of the garden house and lay prostrate completely exhausted by the exertion of dancing. All the followers of Caitanya were now feasted with the delicious Prasād of Jagannāth. Again the car was to move after the Bhog, but it would not, even when pulled by elephants. But when the Master gave it a push, it rattled along. Caitanya and party accompanied the car singing and dancing until it reached the garden of Guṇḍica in the evening and the images were lifted from the car and placed on their thrones.

Jagannāth was to stay in that garden for nine days. The idea behind the procession is that every year Jagannāth, who is none other than Kṛṣṇa, wants to go from Dvārakā to Vṛindāvan where He sported with the Gopas and Gopis.

The garden of Guṇḍica was supposed to be that Vṛndāvan where he would spend these nine days in sporting in the pools and woodlands of that place. This time in the person of the Master he did this actually with the devotees as the inhabitants of Vraja. On the ninth day the Hera-pancami procession of Lakṣmī took place, and after that Jagannāth returned in the car to His usual temple. During this return procession also the Master danced and sang in supreme delight as during the onward drive.

After this, the Navadvip devotees who had already stayed with him for four months at Puri, were ordered by Caitanya to go back home, as they were all house-holders, and as their presence in Bengal was necessary to spread the new Gospel of Vaiṣṇavism he represented. He ordered Nityānanda also to go away to Bengal, with the command that along with Advaita Acārya he should go all over Bengal for the propagation of the Gospel. Caitanya himself continued thereafter to stay at Puri for about three years, every day spending much of his time in singing and dancing before Jagannath. Every year during the time of the car festival the devotees of Navadvip including women, came in large numbers to be benefited by his inspiring company.

**Pilgrimage to Vṛndāvan**

After the stay of three years at Puri he began to express a desire to go to Vṛndāvan, the spot of Kṛṣṇa's divine play. He also wanted to take his bath in the Gaṅgā and meet his mother Śaci at Navadvip on his way to Vṛndāvan. He therefore left Puri with a small entourage of devoted followers. Up to the northern border of Orissa all arrangements for the stay and boarding of the party was made at the order of King Pratāpa Rudra, but at the border he had to cross a turbulent river and pass through the country of a fanactical and wine-sipping Muslim ruler. Thanks to the inspiring personality and electrifying devotion of Caitanya, the border guards of the Muslim ruler became devotees, and helped him in his onward journey. Then he passed through Bengal territory to the bank of Gaṅgā and proceeded in a boat, halting at Pānihāṭi and Kāmārhāṭi on the way. In all those places thousands of people thronged to meet him and the frenzy of devotion spread from him to the crowds like a contagious influence. Proceeding further, he halted at Śāntipur and stayed in Advaita Ācārya's house for ten days. He also met his mother there and assuaged her grief. He prostrated at her feet and holding them, entreated her to permit him to go to Vṛndāvan. The permission was given. He then returned to Puri and after a short stay there, started for Vṛndāvan.

His path lay through the forests of Cotā-Nāgpūr infested by wild beasts and equally wild men. He was accompanied only by one attendant, one Bālcandra Bhattācārya, who procured food stuffs and cooked it for him wherever possible. In this trip he turned wild men into Vaiṣṇavas. Still more wonderful it was that in his presence tigers and stags licked each other in amity and wild animals walked in line by his side. Elephants which came to the pools where he was bathing, when sprinkled with water, began to dance trumpeting Kṛṣṇa's name. Peacocks and other birds, on seeing him, proceeded in his company singing Kṛṣṇa's name and dancing. At Jarkand he saved the ruffianly bearish tribes of that place by teaching them faith in Kṛṣṇa. Thus he travelled through forests enjoying the glorious scenery and without experiencing any of the usual hardships and dangers of such travel, until he reached Kāśī (Banares).

## At Banares

He stayed there for ten days with a devotee Tapan Miśra whom he met at Maṇikarṇikā Ghāt. There was a proud Advaita Sannyāsin called Prakāśānanda there, who had in earlier days sent some scurrilous letters to Caitanya while he was at Puri. The news of Caitanya's presence at Banares was brought to Prakāśānanda by a devoted Brāhmaṇa who described him to Prakāśānanda thus: "A

Sannyāsin has come here from Jagannāth whose glory and power I cannot adequately describe. He is big of limbs, fair as the fairest gold, long armed, lotus-eyed, endowed with all the marks of Godhead as one can see. Whoever beholds him, chants Kṛṣṇa's name. All the marks of a great Bhāgavata described in the Bhāgavata Purāṇa are evidenced in him. Ever does his tongue sing Kṛṣṇa's name and his eyes run tears like the Ganges stream. Now he dances, now laughs, now sings, now weeps or at others roars like a lion. He is named Kṛṣṇa Caitanya. To see him is to know him as fashioned in God's mould." The philosopher Prakāśānanda only laughed and scoffed at all this description, and called this new arrival not a Sannyāsin but a wizard. He dismissed the whole report with the remark that his stock-in-trade of sentimentality will not sell at Kāśī, the seat of Vedānta. Caitanya did not take notice of Prakāśānanda now, but reserved him for his return journey.

He proceeded to Allahabad or Prayāga, where he bathed at the holy Triveṇi. The sight of the Yamuna filled him with Kṛṣṇa consciousness, impelling him to jump recklessly into that fast flowing river.

**At Brindavan**

After a stay of three days there he proceeded to Mathura, the birth place of Śrī Kṛṣṇa. At the sight of the city itself he was in an ecstasy of devotion. The whole period of his stay was one of dancing, singing and entering into trances. He had here the surprising experience of meeting a Brāhmaṇa devotee who had been initiated into the devotional cult by Mādhavendra Purī, the preceptor of Īśvara Purī, his own Master. From him Caitanya learned that Mādhavendra Purī had recovered the concealed image of Gopal and installed it on Govardhana hill. He bathed at Viśram Ghat and worshipped Keśava's image at the place of His nativity. He visited all holy places at Mathura and neighbourhood like Madhu-vana, Tālvana, Kumuda, Bahuda etc. As he passed through, the cows grazing by the way side surrounded him, lowing loudly and licked his limbs tenderly. Herds of deer gazed at his face, licked his body and followed him fearlessly. Black birds and bees sang sweetly on seeing him. The peacocks strutted dancing before him. At his coming trees and creepers put forth sprouts and shed honey like tears of joy. Branches laden with flowers and fruits bowed to his feet, as one hastens to greet a friend with presents. Singing Kṛṣṇa's name, he danced all the way. His passion of devotion on the way to Vṛndāvan grew tenfold of what it had been at Puri. It increased a thousandfold more when he reached Mathura and roamed through the woods of Vṛndāvan. This was in November 1515 when he was about 29.

Historically speaking, modern Vṛndāvan, as Jadunāth Sirkār says, is the creation of the three Gosvāmīs, Rūpa, his brother Sanātana and their nephew Jīva, who were disciples and later contemporaries of Caitanya. They were also the great savants who formulated the philosophy of Acintya-Bhedābheda, the main intellectual support of Caitanya's faith. For Caitanya, even from his Navadvip days the mystical Vṛndāvan was the dreamland that haunted his thoughts. So in 1509 he had sent a disciple Loknāth Cakravarti as the vanguard for the renewal of Vṛndāvan of Kṛṣṇa's days, which had in the passing of time been reduced to jungles. Even when Caitanya visited the place in 1515, the place had not developed much. His visit must have helped to identify the holy spots associated with Śrī Kṛṣṇa. Subsequently it was possible for the three Gosvāmīs and the Vaiṣṇavas coming from Bengal, to develop Vṛndāvan, especially after Raja Mān Singh, the general and a Governor of Emperor Akbar, began to extend his patronage.

Caitanya's stay at Vṛndāvan was short, extending for only a few months. He visited many of the holy spots there like Rādhā-kuṇḍa, Govardhan, Govinda-kuṇḍa, Kanya forest, Kāliya lake, Lauhavana, Gokula etc. Everywhere he sang, danced and imparted Kṛṣṇa-prem to devotees. Life there was however beset with one danger for him. The sight of Yamunā was very often impelling him to throw himself into that rapid stream. His companions had to rescue him several times, and so they felt it was dangerous to permit him to stay on in Vṛndāvan longer. After a few months' stay, they therefore tactfully managed to persuade him to return to Prayāga (Allahabad).

**At Prayāga**

On the way they were threatened to be arrested by a party of six Pathan Muslim troopers under the idea tnat they were robbers. But by the Master's touch the Pathans were transformed into ecstatic devotees of Krsna. One of them, a Pir, became Rāmdās. All became Vairagis and came to be known as Pathan Vaiṣṇavas.

Reaching Prayāga, he stayed there tor ten days, every day bathing in the holy Triveṇi and singing and dancing in the temple of Veṇi-mādhava. During his stay here, he met at the village of Ārali, seven miles away from Triveṇi, Vallaba Bhatta (Ācārya), the well-known founder of the Vaiṣṇava school of Puṣṭi-mārga, and had intimate association with him.

It was here again that he met and instructed his two important disciples, Rūpa and Sanātana, who were to be his foremost apostles to formulate the philosophical structure of his doctrine of Prema-bhakti. These two learned men, coming from aristocratic families, were the ministers of the Muslim ruler of Bengal. By Caitanya's grace they got themselves released from this service, and gathered at his feet to be inspired with Kṛṣṇa-prem. It was Rūpa that could get his release first and reach Caitanya at Prayāga. Realising that he was going to be the future apostle of his church, Caitanya imparted to him many of the fundamental doctrines of his Vaiṣṇavism.

**Instructions to Rūpa Gosvāmī**

Among the teachings that Caitanya imparted to him, some are as follows: "True devotion to Kṛṣṇa is the rarest thing in the universe. In this Samsāra countless beings pass through 84 lakhs of births. Among these there are the animate and the inanimate. Among the former are numerous classes like birds, beasts, water-born creatures etc, human beings forming but a very small minority. Among men the largest section are either too barbarous or extremely worldly minded. A few think of God. Among them, most are devoted to Karma (ritualistic duties), some to Knowledge. Among a million devoted to Knowledge, hardly one is liberated, and among those liberated, one in a million alone is found to be truly devoted to Kṛṣṇa. For, the true devotee of Kṛṣṇa is passionless and tranquil. While the others covet enjoyment, salvation or psychic powers, Kṛṣṇa's devotees care only for whole-hearted service of Him with body, mind and soul in an absolutely selfless spirit. In the minds of those who care for salvation and other self-centred fulfilments, true love of Kṛṣṇa can never be kindled. From the culture of Bhakti, ardour is born. When ardour deepens, it is called Prema or Love.

As Prema grows it is successively called Sneha, Māna, Praṇaya Rāga, Anurāga, Bhāva and Mahābhāva. When the spiritual (Sāttvika) and extensive (Vyabhicārī) emotions mingle, love of Kṛṣṇa becomes a veritable nectar in taste. In different types of Bhaktas, the inclination (Rati) assumes five different forms, namely, the Śānta (the placid), the Dāsya (that of servantship), the Sakhya (comradely), Vātsalya (parental) and Madhura (cōnjugal). Again the ardour (Rati) for Kṛṣṇa is of two kinds, the first accompanied by sense of His Godhead, and the second pure and simple. At Gokula, Kṛṣṇa displayed Himself free from His Godhead aspect, while at Mathura, Dvārakā, Vaikuṇṭha etc,. His Godhead is more conspicuous. Where the sense of His Godhead is predominant, love for Him is contracted, whereas the way of pure ardour is to disregard Godhead even when it is openly shown. In the Śānta and Dāsya emotions the former consciousness is a little kindled, but in the Vātsalya, Sakhya and Madhura it is shrunken. The pure love called unmixed (Kevala) ignores His divinity, and whenever it does recognise Him as Power, the intensity of the loving connection with him diminishes.

"Devotion to Kṛṣṇa and conquest of desires are the marks of all these types of devotees. A Śānta votary's attachment is like an odourless flower. He has acquired only a true sense of God's nature as the Supreme Spirit and Divinity. The Dāsya mood better develops the cognition of Kṛṣṇa as the Lord of all powers and constantly gratifies Him by serving Him with a sense of His divinity and with honour and great glorification. It has got the merits of Śānta plus service. The Sakhya Rasa possesses got the merit plus absolute trust in Kṛṣṇa, and service is characterised by reliance and free camaraderie without any inhibition of awe. So this has three qualities, including the two former. In Vātsalya or parental love there are the above three qualities plus tenderness. Such a devotee looks on Kṛṣṇa as the *protege* and himself as His patron. It has therefore four qualities and is like nectar. In the Madhura mood all the above qualities are present and in addition to them the votary serves Kṛṣṇa as a lover, offering him his or her own person. In this all the earlier four characteristics are synthesised into a complexion of its own in the form of Ātma-samarpaṇa. (complete resignation of the self)."

**At Banares Again: Instructing Sanātana**

After giving these teachings to Rūpa, the Master started for Kāśī (Banares). He also gave him the command that he should now go to Vṛndāvan, and after his (Caitanya's) return to Puri, go to meet him there.

At Kāśī, Caitanya stayed at the house of Tapaṇ Miśra as before. Shortly after his arrival, Sanātana, who managed to escape from the clutches of his Muslim Navāb, reached Kāśī and met Caitanya. Recognising in him the competency to be an apostle of his school, Caitanya gave him some of the most profound teachings of his brand of Vaiṣṇavism, just as he did to Rūpa. Some of these may be summarised as follows: "The soul (Jīva) is the eternal servant of Kṛṣṇa. Kṛṣṇa has three inherent powers. Cit-Power (Consciousness), Jīva-power and Māyā-power. If the Jīva, which is in the middle (Taṭastha), looks at Kṛṣṇa, he is uplifted by the Cit-power, if he turns himself away from Kṛṣṇa, Māyā-power entangles him in Samsāra. The scripture, the Guru and introspection lead the Jīva to Kṛṣṇa. For this, Kṛṣṇa has revealed the Vedas and the Purāṇas. The Veda treats of Relation, Epithet and Needs. Relation is the attainment of Kṛṣṇa and Faith is the means for this. Epithets are His names. Service of Kṛṣṇa in the Madhura or conjugal form of love is the need or the supreme achievement for man. By serving Him thus we can attain the Relish (Rasa), of which He is the embodiment. The fruit of love is not wealth or freedom from rebirth but the beatitude that service gives.

"Kṛṣṇa in His all-embracing form dwells in the Parama-Vyoma (the Highest Space). There are endless Vaikuṇṭhas which form His retinue only. Ānanda (Bliss) inspired by Cit (Consciousness) fills the Vaikuṇṭhas. Kṛṣṇa's attributes are countless. The mind fails to comprehend His exploits. See how at one and the same time he created the natural and super-natural cowherds and kine, as described in the Bhāgavata. The millions of calves, cow-boys all assumed the form of the four-armed Lord of Vaikuṇṭha, each with a separate universe and a Brahmā adoring Him.

The Brahmā Samhitā declares that Kṛṣṇa Himself is the unequalled Supreme Deity. It means that Mahā-Viṣṇu, Padmanābha, and Kṣīrodaka-śāyin, who are the three Puruṣa incarnations and causes of the universe and of all beings, are mere particles (Amśas) of Kṛṣṇa. This is only the superficial interpretation.

"Its esoteric meaning is that Kṛṣṇa has three abodes Antaḥpura, Goloka and Vṛndāvana. In the last He ever dwells with his parents, comrades etc. Here His sweet attributes, tenderness, mercy etc., are manifested to the full and Rāsa and other exploits take place. Below his eternal Abode, the universes are endless. Every universe has its own Brahmā the creator. It is said that once when Brahmā came to Dvāraka to pay obeisance to Kṛṣṇa and was introduced by the porter, Kṛṣṇa asked which Brahmā he was. Brahmā, who was under the idea that he was the only one of that designation and the universe he created was the only universe, was surprised at the query, and wanted to know what Kṛṣṇa meant by it. Then Kṛṣṇa by an act of will brought out a procession of Brahmās presiding over innumerable universes. Such is the glory of Kṛṣṇa. It is for this reason that the Vedas declare Kṛṣṇa to be the Supreme Being Himself.

Śraddhā is what has to be attained (Abhidheya). Śraddhā means firm and unquestioning faith in Kṛṣṇa. Those who have Śraddhā are qualified for Bhakti. There are different grades of Bhakti according to differences of ardour and passion. There are sixty four modes of cultivating Bhakti. Of these the most important five are: 1) society of holy men 2) Kīrtan or devotional chanting of Kṛṣṇa's name 3) listening to the reading of the Bhāgavata 4) dwelling at Mathura i.e. a holy place associated with Kṛṣṇa. 5) Reverential service of his image. The man who, renouncing desires, seeks complete shelter in Kṛṣṇa, the only one worthy of such seeking, is not indebted to Gods, Ṛṣis or the Manes. He who adores Kṛṣṇa abandoning Śāstric duties and rites, feels nevertheless no temptation for forbidden sinful ways. Theological knowledge and monasticism are not essential for development of Bhakti.

"The final fruit of Bhakti is Prema (unmotivated love). Bhakti has its intrinsic (Svarūpa) and extrinsic (peripheral) forms. The man with Śraddhā (Faith) associates with pious men. Such association gives occasion for the hearing and chanting of Kṛṣṇa's name and development of Ruci (Taste) for the same, Ruci develops into inclination (Āsakti), which is the sprout of passion for Kṛṣṇa in the soul. When this emotion deepens, it takes the name of Prema, which is the ultimate fruit and the source of every form of bliss.

"Now hear the characteristics of one who has developed Rati. No worldly affliction can disturb the mind of such a person. He never wastes his time but always communes with Kṛṣṇa. No sensual gratification attracts him nor worldly success elates him. He is a picture of dignified humility and of passionate longing for Kṛṣṇa.

"As Prema for Kṛṣṇa develops, it takes the forms of Sneha, Māna, Praṇaya, Rāga, Anurāga, Bhāva and Mahābhāva — just as from the one source of sugarcane juice we have molasses, brown sugar, yellow sugar-candy and white sugar-candy. As these grow purer and purer, the resulting forms increase in deliciousness (Rasa), so do the above stages in the development of love. This Rasa is of five kinds - Śānta, Dāsya, Sakhya, Vātsalya, and Madhura.

"Kṛṣṇa, the darling of Vraja's lord, is the chief of lovers while lady Rādhā is at the head of Mistresses. Countless are the qualities of Rādhā and Kṛṣṇa.

"The topic of Rasa has been expounded by me elaborately to your brother Rūpa. Now you too go to Vṛndāvan and prepare the sacred code (Smṛti) of Vaiṣṇavas, discover the lost holy spots and shrines at Mathura and Vṛndāvan, and preach the Gospel of Bhakti in all ways."

**Prakāśānanda's Conversion**

Caitanya stayed about two months at Banares at Tapan Miśra's quarters. Besides giving elaborate instructions to

Sanātana on the Vaiṣṇava doctrine, an important achievement of his on this occasion was the discomfiture and conversion of Prakāśānanda, the doyen of Advaitism, in that city of learning. He could also popularise Bhakti and the study of the Bhāgavata among Sannyāsins who were till then devoted exclusively to the doctrines elaborated in Śrī Śaṅkara's commentaries. Prakāśānanda had earlier been in the habit of reviling at Caitanya as a mere wizard or mesmerist. But when confronted with the Master at a meeting arranged by a devotee, Prakāśānanda felt completely overcome by the majesty of the former's personality and the cogency of his expositions. He abandoned his Advaita ideology and became a disciple of Caitanya. He was renamed Prabodhānanda and asked to go to Vṛndāvan and preach the Bhakti doctrine. He wrote many works, the most important of which is *Caitanya Candrāmṛta.*

Prakāśānanda's conversion and the sight of Caitanya's ecstatic Kīrtan parties accompanied with dancing and singing of Hari-kīrtan produced a revolution in the attitude of the Sannyāsins of Banares towards the Bhakti doctrine, to which they were made to turn from the exclusive study of Śrī Śaṅkara's commentaries. He preached to them that the meaning of the Vedānta Sūtras of Bādarāyaṇa is best understood through the commentary on it by Bādarāyaṇa himself and not through some one else who twists their meaning to suit his philosophy. The Bhāgavata Purāṇa which Bādarāyaṇa himself composed is the correct interpretation of the Vedānta Sūtras, and the Sannyāsins were exhorted to study the Bhāgavata carefully. Bhāgavata is the fountain of Bhakti in which the supremacy of Kṛṣṇa is glorified. Large numbers of people in and around Banares were converted into the Bhakti doctrine by the presence of Caitanya and his Kīrtans in that region.

**Back to Puri**

After accomplishing this great mission in Banares, Caitanya walked away one night with a solitary companion back to Nīlācal via the forest of Jharkand regıon. His arrival at Puri came to be known in and around Puri and all his old devotees began to gather in the place. The news reached his home town at Nadia and other places of Bengal. A large party of pilgrims from Bengal also arrived. It became a practice thereafter for these Bengali devotees to go to Puri every year near about the Car Festival time, take part in the devotional programmes of the occasion and return after a stay of four months at Puri. Sometime women too came with the party, and among them was his mother Śaci also. From other provinces also devotees who heard of Caitanya's greatness came to Puri, but many could not do so, and for their benefit he sent competent disciples, inspired by Kṛṣṇa-prema, as missionaries, just as he had done with Nityānanda in regard to Bengal. As for himself he finally settled down at Puri at the age of thirty (1455), spending his time in constant adoration of Jagannāth. He did not go out anywhere afterwards. There he gave Darśan (audience) to the numerous devotees who flocked to see him.

**Sanātana at Puri**

One such missionary was Sanātana Gosvāmī, whom he had already instructed at Prayāga (Allahabad) and sent to Vṛndāvan. He now came to Puri via Jharkand forest to meet Caitanya again. The travails of this difficult journey brought on him an almost unbearable skin disease. So on reaching Puri he decided to end his life by allowing himself to be crushed under the wheels of the Car of Jagannāth during the time of the car festival. When he met Caitanya, the latter divined his suicidal intention and spoke to him thus: "Sanātana! If giving up life could have made one gain Kṛṣṇa, I could have sacrificed my life a million times over in a moment. It is not by courting death but by adoration that we can gain Him. There is no other way. Suicide and the like are born of Tamas, and are sinful. Among methods of adoration, the chief are the nine kinds of Bhakti spoken of in the Bhāgavata, and of these Nāma-saṅkīrtan or chanting of the divine Name has the highest place."

Then Sanātana replied, "You are omniscient like God. I move like a wooden machine as you turn the handle. I am a lowly wretch, wicked in disposition. What would you gain by keeping me alive?" At this Caitanya said "Your body is my property. You have given yourself up to me. How dare you think of destroying what is another's property? Can't you distinguish between a crime and a just deed? Your body is my chief instrument. With it I shall carry out my purposes. The exposition of the nature of devotion, the devotee and Kṛṣṇa-prema, the codifying of the duties and daily practices of Vaiṣṇavas, preaching the supremacy of devotion to Kṛṣṇa and of love for Kṛṣṇa's service, the restoration of forgotten holy places at Mathura and Vṛndāvan, the teaching of true asceticism, the preaching of this faith at Mathura and Vṛndāvan which are my favourite places — all these I direct you to do. By my mother's command I live at Nīlācal (Puri) instead of at Vṛndāvan, and therefore I cannot preach at Mathura in person. Your body is the means by which I want to do all these works. And you want to give it up! How can I allow it?" Sanātana bowed down in acceptance of the Master's command. Sanātana's body was covered with running sores and eruptions, but Caitanya embraced him, and lo! the eruptions disappeared and his body assumed a golden hue. After *dol-yātrā* festival, he was sent to Vṛndāvan with detailed instructions as to what he should do.

**Humbling of Vallabha Bhatta**

Another noteworthy incident that took place in these days was the humbling of Vallabha Bhatta's (Ācārya's) pride and his conversion. Vallabha was the well-known founder of the Puṣṭi-mārga which is mainly based on the teachings of the Bhāgavata. He had contacted Caitanya sometime back at Allahabad and was full of admiration for his devotional fervour. So on meeting him at Puri, Vallabha made humble obeisance to him. Caitanya immediately came to understand that though the Bhatta was a great devotee of Viṣṇu, he was mightily proud of his learning, and that God had sent him there to humble his pride of scholarship. So Caitanya at first in all humility informed the Bhatta that he was not learned enough to discourse with him and undertook to introduce him to some of his learned disciples. An assembly of learned Vaiṣṇavas headed by Advaita Ācārya was next day called and introduced to the Bhatta who was very much impressed by their Vaiṣṇava effulgence. Soon after, the Car Festival took place in which the Master and his followers performed their grand Kīrtan and devotional dance. The Bhatta was spell-bound to see and hear all that. Next he went to Caitanya and told him that he was writing a commentary on the Bhāgavata and would like to read some portions of it to him. Caitanya professed his incapacity to understand such profound writings and referred him to Advaita Ācārya.

So the Bhatta went frequently to Advaita and read his commentary to him, but was always rebuffed, as Advaita slighted his writings, pointing out several mistakes in them. One day the Bhatta remarked to the Ācārya: "According to the accepted custom of the noble born, no wife will utter the name of her husband. In your philosophy you teach that Kṛṣṇa is the husband of all, and yet you advocate the loud uttering of His name. Is it not incongruous?" The Ācārya replied: "Well, Kṛṣṇa is the husband of all, and he has commanded us all, His wives, to chant His name in the Bhāgavata. Now no chaste wife will disobey the command of her husband. So we are chanting Kṛṣṇa's name." To the Bhatta this came like a powerful blow on the hood of the serpent of pride in him. Another day he boasted to Caitanya himself that in his commentary on the Bhāgavata he has differed very much from the interpretations of Śrīdhara Svāmī, the celebrated exegetist, and refuted his teachings. Caitanya with a pun on 'Svāmī' remarked: "One who does not follow (her) Svāmī (husband) is ranked among harlots."

All these experiences brought Vallabha to his senses. Reflection made him understand his own stupidity in assuming such an attitude of scholarly pride before a divine personality like Caitanya. So next day he went and prostrated himself before Caitanya in an attitude of true humility and was about to place Caitanya's feet on his head. Caitanya checked him and said: "You are a scholar and a devotee at the same time. When these two qualities are present, pride should not exist. But you say you have written a commentary in scorn of Śrīdhara Svāmī. I understand the Bhāgavata through Śrīdhara Svāmī. He is the world's Guru — my Guru. Your writing contrary to Śrīdhara is mere labour lost; no one will accept it. So write a commentary in his footsteps. Leave off your pride and adore the Lord Śrī Kṛṣṇa, and you will soon attain to Kṛṣṇa's feet."

The Bhatta was till now the worshipper of child Kṛṣṇa. Now with the Master's permission he took from Gadādhar Paṇḍita initiation in the Mantra and ceremonials for the adoration of youthful Kṛṣṇa in Madhura-bhāva.*

## The Evening of His Life

The last thirteen (according to some fourteen) years of Caitanya from the age of thirty were spent exclusively at Puri. During this time he was continuously attended upon by Raghunāth-dās and Svarūp Dāmodar. Beyond what has been mentioned in the above paragraphs, there are not many

* This account of the humbling of Vallabha, who was the promulgator of the wide-spread Puṣṭi-mārga, may be coloured by sectarian jealousy. In the accounts of Vallabha's life by his followers, no such humbling is mentioned, although they give a description of the meeting between these great teachers in genuine cordiality.

incidents to narrate. He spent all his time in adoration of Jagannāth. It was also a period of protracted love-sickness, in which he felt himself to be Rādhā feeling intense pangs of separation from Kṛṣṇa now, and next experiencing the ecstasy of union with Him, and again losing Him and pining for Him. For long periods he was not in his usual consciousness, and behaved like one living in a world of apparent fantasy, in which the realm of Kṛṣṇa's love sports at Vṛndāvan was more real to him than the world in which his physical body was being experienced by his devotee attendants.

In these moods his behaviour looked like those of one mad to men who lived in material consciousness and could have no entry into the spiritual awareness in which he was absorbed. He raved day and night identifying himself with Rādhā, pining for Kṛṣṇa. Sometimes in agony he rubbed his face on the floor causing laceration and profuse bleeding. One night when he tried to rush out of his room in a frenzy, he dashed himself against the walls of his room and sustained serious injuries.

What looks like a strange and remarkable miracle that took place during this period of his life, is reported in Caitanya-caritāmṛta. One night he was missing from his room, the exit door of which was blocked by his sleeping attendant. When the disciples noticed this and began a search, they found his body lying unconscious in a strange condition. It was elongated into six cubits with only a thin case of skin connecting the neck and the limbs with the trunk. The frightened disciples began to chant the name of Kṛṣṇa loudly in his ears, which made him slightly conscious and soon get up with a *Hari-bōl.* The body shrank and the limbs were all united with the trunk in to its normal shape.

Another day he ran in a frenzied mood with the speed of wind to the Chatak hillock, taking it to be Govardhan hill. The disciples Raghunāth Dās and Svarūp Dāmodar who went in hot pursuit found his body lying dead on the ground. It had become stiff and incapable of movement. Every part of the skin had swollen like a boil, the hair stood on end like Kadamba flower, and blood oozed with sweat. When the disciples chanted Kṛṣṇa's name in his ears, he again became conscious and addressed them thus: "You have brought me back here from Govardhan. You have snatched me away from viewing Kṛṣṇa's Līlā among the herds of cows and calves, with Rādhā and her handmaids on Govardhan hill. Why have you brought me away from there, only to cause me grief?" So saying he began to weep in disconsolate grief. Thus the realm of devotional ideology was more real to him than the work-a-day world of earth-bound souls.

**Caught in the Fisherman's Net**

Another day, without anybody's knowledge he went to the sea-side. Seeing the blue ocean, his idealised vision took it for the blue Yamunā river in which Kṛṣṇa sported with the Gopis. He rushed into the sea and was carried away by the waves. His attendants, who went in anxious search of him, came across a fisherman with his net on his shoulders, laughing, weeping, dancing and chanting Hari! Hari! The devotees stopped him and questioned him anxiously whether he had seen any man there and why he was in such a mood. He replied, "I have not seen any man there. But a dead body was caught in my net, and I carefully dragged it ashore thinking it might be a big fish. But on seeing that it was only a corpse, I was frightened. While cleaning the net I touched that bloated body and at once the spirit of the dead entered into me and I have been reduced to this state. The body lay like a corpse with a fixed stare in the eye, but at times it groaned, at others it remained inert. I am in search of an exorcist to rid me of this possession."

The fisherman then guided the devotees to the so-called corpse, which was none but Śrī Kṛṣṇa Caitanya. They beheld him lying on the ground, huge-bodied, pale-skinned and coated with sea-sand. His limbs were abnormally long, loose and with skin flapping. They brought the body to a dry spot and cleaned it and then began to loudly sing Kṛṣṇa-kīrtans into his ear. Gradually he came to consciousness and stood up in his natural form. Then he began speaking to the devotees in a complaining tone: "Beholding the Yamunā (meaning the ocean), I went to Vṛndāvan and then found Vraja's darling sporting in the water with Rādhā and the other Gopis. I stood on the bank gazing at the scene while one of the Sakhīs (female comrades) pointed out the mysteries to me. My heart was filled with bliss at the sight; just then you have caught hold of me and with great noise brought me here. Ah! where is the Yamunā? Where Vṛndāvana? Where Kṛṣṇa? And Where the milk maids? You have destroyed that bliss."

**Last Message**

In such unheard-of transports of intense devotion, with alternating moods of union and separation as Rādhā had, he spent his last years at Puri. Towards the close of his life he gave the following charge to his devotee attendants. "Listen Svarūp and Rāmānanda Roy!" The Supreme healer in this Iron Age is the Saṅkīrtan of Kṛṣṇa's name. It is equivalent to Vedic sacrifice, and the true sacrificer in it is rewarded with Kṛṣṇa's feet. Saṅkīrtan enables us to conquer sin and the world. It creates purity of soul. Chant the name at meals, in bed, here, there, everywhere. It is not restricted to any place or time — it works everywhere. It bears the name of Sarva-śakti (omnipotence).

"Listen, Rāmānanda, to the way in which the name should be recited in order to develop a passion for it. The devotee, if high of rank, should regard himself as lowly like the grass. He should learn patience from the tree which does not cry out even when it is cut-down and which does not beg for water even when it is perishing at drought, but on the other hand gives away its possession to all who ask of it, bears sun and rain itself but protects others from them. The Vaiṣṇava, however high, should be free from pride; he should venerate all forms of life as animated by Kṛṣṇa.. Take Kṛṣṇa's name thus and you will be inspired with Prema." He recited to them eight verses of his own composition on different moods of Bhakti, which run as follows;

*Ceto-darpaṇa-mārjanam bhava-mahā-dāvāgni-*
*nirvāpaṇam*
*śreyaḥ-kairava-candrikā-vitaraṇam*
*vidyā-vadhū-jīvanam /*
*ānand'āmbudhi-vardhanam pratipadam*
*purṇ'āmṛtāsvādanam*
*sarvātma-snapanam param vijayate*
*Śrī Kṛṣṇa-saṅkīrtanam // 1*

Hail unto the hymning of Kṛṣṇa's holy Name —
A detergent that cleanses the mirror of our minds,
A down-pour that totally extinguishes the forest fire of
worldly woes,
A beneficence spreading the moonlight that brings to bloom
the lily of supreme good,
The life-breath that sustains the Bride of Enlightenment,
The hightide that swells the level of the sea of Bliss,
A veritable nectar flowing from every syllable,
A bath that cools every fibre of our being.

*Nāmnām akāri bahudhā nija-sarva-śaktis*
*tatr'ārpitā niyamitaḥ smaraṇe na kālaḥ /*
*etādṛśī tava kṛpā bhagavan mam'āpi*
*durdaivam īdṛśam ih'ājani n'ānurāgaḥ // 2*

Thou, with numerous names, hast infused all Thy divine
power into them,
And Thou hast put no restrictions too on the time for their
chanting.
But, O Lord, even when so abundant is Thy grace,
No taste I find in me for them, the luckless creature that
I am.

*Tṛṇād api sunīcena, taror api sahiṣṇunā /*
*amāninā mānadena, kīrtanīyaḥ sadā Harih // 3*

Hari, the Supreme Lord, becomes the object of
remembrance to him
Who feels himself humbler than a blade of grass,
Who remains more patient than a tree in weathering all
the storms of life,
And who honours all beings without any feeling of
self-importance.

*Na dhanam na janam na sundarīm*
*kavitām vā jagadīśa kāmaye /*
*mama janmani janman'īśvare*
*bhavatād bhaktir ahaitukī tvayi // 4*

I seek not wealth, nor fame, nor pleasure, nor literary
greatness;
What I pray for is that I may have in life after life
Devotion to Thee with no extraneous motive behind.

*Ayi nanda-tanūja kiṅkaram*
*patitam mām viṣame bhav'āmbudhau /*
*kṛpayā tava pāda-paṅkaja-*
*sthita-dhūlī-sadṛśam vicintaya // 5*

O son of Nanda! I Thy servant am drowning in the
treacherous sea of transmigration.
May Thou have mercy to make me adhere to Thy lotus
feet like a speck of dust.

*Nayanam galad-aśru-dhārayā*
*vadanam gadgada-ruddhayā girā /*
*pulakair nicitam vapuḥ kadā*
*tava nāma-grahaṇe bhaviṣyati // 6*

When shall that state come on me —
The state in which at the very utterance of Thy name
The eyes become flooded with flowing tears,

The speech arrested by choked-up voice,
And the body motionless and covered with horripilation!

As Radha soliloquises:

*Yugāyitam nimeṣeṇa*
*cakṣuṣā prāvṛṣāyitam /*
*śūnyāitam jagat sarvam*
*Govinda-viraheṇa me // 7*

Separation from Govinda makes for me
A moment as endless as an age;
It makes my eyes shed tears as clouds in rainy season;
And the whole world appears to me as a dreary void.

*Āśliṣya vā pādaratām pinaṣṭu mām*
*adarśanāṭ marma hatām karotu vā /*
*yathā tathā vā vidadhātu lampaṭo*
*mat-prāṇa-nāthas tu sa eva n'āparaḥ // 8*

Whether He embraces me or tramples on me who clings to His feet,
Or cuts me to the quick by disappearing from view —
In whatever ways the fickle and frivolous one may torment me,
He alone is the Lord of my heart.

**Unsolved Mystery of His End**

When and how Sri Caitanya passed away are not mentioned by the author of Caitanya-caritāmṛta, who stops his narration abruptly with the Lord's last sermon to disciples. But there are popular beliefs, besides some quasi-historical accounts of it, all of them calculated to throw a veil of mystery over what looks like an unpleasant end. There is a popular belief that he attained absorption with the body itself in the image of Jagannāth or of Gopīnāth. Others hold that Caitanya's drowning himself in the sea marks his end and that the incident of the fisherman rescuing him is a story added to it afterwards by the credulous imagination of devotees. But Kṛṣṇa Dās Kavirāj confirms the rescue story as factual.

The version of Caitanya-Maṅgal of Jayānanda (1511) is this: During the car festival of the month of Āṣāḍha (June-July) in 1533 Caitanya fell down while dancing and had a serious leg injury followed by severe pain and a high rise of temperature. He told his attendant Svarūp Gosvāmī that he would leave the earth next night on the Aṣṭami Tithi. At the predicted time celestial flowers of various colours were thrown in heaps on him from the unseen, and celestials began to sing. Viṣṇu's heavenly chariot with Garuḍa figure on it came and Caitanya's spirit went in it to Viṣṇu's Abode. This took place in the temples of Toha Gopīnātha. The exact day of his demise according to Jādunath Sarkar is 14th June 1533.

Prof. Dinesh Chandra Sen, who has investigated this question of Caitanya's passing, has accepted this version of Caitanya-Maṅgal in the main. According to him death took place by about 3.00 p.m. With the permission of King Pratāpa Rudra, it was decided to bury the body in the premises of Guṇḍica-vādi adjacent to the temple. In a corner near the main pavillion of the temple a spot was cleared by the removal of pavements and the body was buried underneath, taking special care to leave no marks indicative of the burial. The temple was closed to the public for several hours till late at night. This must be the basis of the belief that he passed away at about 10.00 p.m. There is a foot print marked in the Guṇḍica-vihāra, which some presume is the place where the burial must have taken place. But Jādunath Sircār, a noted historian and a devout follower of the Caitanya cult, says in his short monograph on Caitanya's life in his translation of *Caitanya-Caritāmṛta* as follows: 'At last on 14 June 1533, his physical frame broke down under such prolonged mental convulsion and self-inflicted torments, and he passed away under circumstances over which the piety of his biographers has drawn the veil of mystery.'*

This veil of mystery gives credence to a shocking story that Caitanya was murdered by a conspiracy of high officers of the state and a set of jealous and offended priests of the temple — a story accepted by another authority, Ashok Chatterjee Sastri, a critic and scholar of eminence, who is the Head of the Department of Sanskrit at the University of Calcutta. He reviews the various conflicting accounts of Caitanya's end in works in Bengali and Oriya, and he comes to this conclusion, which according to him gets further confirmation from the history of Orissa at that time.

The stories of Caitanya's end are as follows: 1. One day Caitanya went to the temple according to his daily practice, and arriving at the inner sanctum, stood gazing steadfastly at the lustrous face of Jagannāth. Immediately all the temple doors were automatically closed. Caitanya prayed to the Deity and embraced His image and got dissolved into the divine body of Jagannāth. This is the widely believed account of his end. This is mentioned in Locana Dās's Caitanya-Maṅgala with the difference that the incident took place in the neighbouring Guṇḍica-vādi. 2) According to Vṛndāvana Dāsa's Caitanya Bhāgavata also this absorption into Jagannāth is mentioned. But the recently brought out (but hitherto unpublished), chapters of the same work say as follows: Caitanya one day, overpowered by the feeling of separation from Kṛṣṇa, rushed to the sanctum sanctorum to embrace the image, undeterred by the protests of the priests and the worshippers. The priests thereupon rushed after him with sticks in hand. Caitanya then ceased to be visible and went to the temple of Madanagopāla in the disguise of a mendicant. His whereabouts was not known to any one thereafter. Locana Dāsa's Caitanya-Maṅgala also gives the same story but the incident took place not in Jagannāth's temple but at the nearby Guṇḍica-vādi. 3) Jayānanda's Caitanya-maṅgala gives a more rational account. It has been given already earlier, and it has the acceptance of Prof. Dinesh Chandra Sen in the main. 4) According to Bhakti-ratnākara of Narahari Cakravarthy, Caitanya entered the temple of Gopinātha and disappeared therein never to come out again. It was in February 1534. The other view is that his demise took place in July 1533. 5) Vasudeva Dāsa's Caitanya-cakda in Oriya language gives a sensational account of his disappearance. According to him the senseless body of Caitanya was found behind the Garuḍa Pillar in the courtyard of Jagannāth's temple at about 11.00 p.m. As soon as Caitanya 'the moving Jagannāth' entered into the stationary Jagannāth' (i.e. the temple image), all the doors of the temple were closed. 6) Caitanya-Caritāmṛta, the monumental work on Caitanya by Kṛṣṇadās Kavirāj, is absolutely silent on how and when his life ended.

The 'veil of mystery' gives credence to the shocking story that Caitanya was murdered by some jealous priests of Puri Temple with the connivance of certain high officers of State. Prof. Ashok Chatterjee Sastri, currently the

## An Estimate

Thus ended the life of one of the most remarkable personalities that the world has ever seen. He was an intellectual and scholar of the highest order who renounced that gift as a trifle in comparison with the treasure of divine love buried in the heart of man. He has not therefore left any writing beyond the eight verses we have quoted above, but in place of such records, he has left an indelibly engraved record of life on the rock of history which any one who cares for Bhakti can read. His body and mind formed a centre of magnetic power which radiated its energy into all beings that contacted him. Kṛṣṇa-prema is the name of that magnetic power. Bhakti is ridiculed by some

---

Head and Professor of Sanskrit at the University of Calcutta, supports this story and thinks that these conflicting and mystifying accounts of Caitanya's end make one feel they are attempts to hide an unpleasant fact. And Kṛṣṇa Dās Kavirāj's absolute silence in his elaborate account of Caitanya at Puri in his work Caitanya-caritāmṛta is a confirmation of the above surmise. According to Prof. Sastri, Caitanya's end was connected with the contemporary history of Orissa. Pratāpa Rudra, the King of Orissa, began to spend all his time at Puri with Caitanya for his holy association. He therefore neglected the affairs of State even though the State was threatened with invasions by neighbouring powers. This provoked great discontent among his high officers, the nobility, and above all in his commander-in-chief Govindavidyādhara. Their anti-Caitanya attitude coincided with the desire of the priests of Puri Temple who found that the king's favours to them were drying up due to his attachment to Caitanya, and the income from devotees too was dwinding on account of Caitanya's presence there. The coincidence of interests resulted in a conspiracy hatched together by the two offended parties to get rid of Caitanya. One day the temple doors were closed all on a sudden and Caitanya disappeared thereafter — i.e. murdered and buried in the temple premises.

The events that immediately followed Caitanya's demise seem to confirm the surmise. Immediately after Caitanya's end, Pratāpa Rudra left Puri for Katak with his family and all his entourage. So also did all the close attendants and devotees of Caitanya migrate immediately from Puri to Vṛndāvan. Most significantly, the daily Kṛṣṇa-Kīrtana that was going on in the temple during Caitanya's days was totally stopped for fifty years.

We would like to add that temple priests have been found to be up to such heinous acts when their income and influence are seriously affected. When Rāmānuja took charge of Śrīraṅgam temple and made reforms in its management, the priests made an attempt to poison him. Fortunately the attempt was foiled.

intellectuals as vapid and insubstantial sentimentalism. But in Caitanya it was solidly substantial and at the same time irresistibly penetrative. However intellectual and strong-willed a man might be, Caitanya could soften him with the water of Kṛṣṇa-prema and thus make him pliable like clay in his hand.

Bhakti in his teaching bifurcates from the sentiment of awe which is a result of a vivid sense of divine majesty as the All-creator, and takes the form of Prema. When the sentiment of awe arising from the perception of God as the All-creator is completely submerged by the awareness of Him as embodiment of Blissfulness (Ānanda-svarūpa), then Bhakti becomes pure love, Prema. Prema is characterised by a sense of 'Ownness' with regard to the object of love. Thereby it eliminates all inhibition in one's mind in respect of His All-powerfulness and seeks one's fulfilment in serving Him — the dearest of the dear — without expectation of any return.

Kṛṣṇa with countless auspicious attributes, is for Caitanya that Archetypal divine form on which man's whole-hearted affection should be centred. This affection, being personalised, takes the colouring of all forms of human love, but resembles it only in form and not in content. It is not a sublimation of human affection; on the contrary human affections are a distortion of it. Unlike other Vaiṣṇava Ācāryas, Caitanya advocated the conjugal form of love. Rādhā of the Vaiṣṇava Purāṇas is the model of it. When a royal minister, who lived an active life in the world, asked him whether there was any way of salvation for such a person like himself, Caitanya replied: "As an immoral woman thinks of her illicit lover while living in the midst of her family, so do thou silently and ceaselessly meditate on Hari while doing your earthly work."

This universal prescription of conjugal attitude is the special feature of Caitanya's teachings unlike those of other Vaiṇava Ācāryas who speak of it only in hesitant terms, perhaps fearing that it would lead to antinomism. But Caitanya illustrated by his rigid ascetic life that this sentiment he advocated was the antipodes of sexuality. He eschewed every form of comfort and contacts with the opposite sex. He never even allowed women devotees to come near him. They could see him only standing at a distance. Some of his disciples who made slight deviations from this discipline were mercilessly excommunicated by him. This strict avoidance of sexuality in life in any form while teaching and practising Kāma-bhakti of the illicit type — an ideal of which Caitanya himself set a glowing example — was followed to the letter in the lives of his immediate successors, the six Gosvāmīs of Vṛndāvan and other devotees at Nadia.

But as decades passed and time made the memories of these examples dimmer and dimmer in the minds of devotees, antinomism did set in among the followers of the Caitanya sect in the form of the cults of Sahajīyas, Karta-bhājas, Vairāgi-Vairāgiṇīs etc. Association of women even in extra-marital relationship became the common feature of these degenerate sects, bringing much disrespect to the great devotional movement. But with the progress of the 19th Century, enlightened public criticism has improved matters. Above all it has spread to the Western countries by the missionary enterprise of the leaders of the Kṛṣṇa consciousness-movement, known as Iskcon. Thus the momentum of Caitanya's effort at converting Prema-bhakti into a mass movement has expanded from the boundaries of India into foreign lands.

**After Caitanya**

Vṛndāvan in the North, Bengal in the East with Navadvip as the centre, and Puri in the south-east became the main seats of Caitanya Vaiṣṇavism. This generated some shades of difference in the faith that developed in these regions. In Vṛndāvan Caitanya had left six learned men as Gosvāmīs (Fathers of the Church) — these being Rūpa,

Sanātana and their nephew Jīva, besides Gopāla Bhatta, Raghunātha Bhatta and Raghunātha-dāsa. A personage equally important as these, but not a contemporary of Caitanya was Kṛṣṇadās Kavirāja, a disciple of the last mentioned of the Gosvāmī's and the author of the famous Bengali work Caitanya-Caritāmrta on Caitanya's life and teachings, which has become the most influential and widely read scripture of the sect. Rūpa, Sanātana and Jīva were great Sanskrit scholars and trained philosophers, and their works, which are all in Sanskrit, formulated the Acintya-bhedā-bheda philosophy and the Kṛṣṇa theology, which form the support and intellectual structure of Caitanya's Vaiṣṇavism. Kṛṣṇa and his Śaktis and their relation form the subject of their disquisitions, although the divinity of Caitanya is fully recognised. The Gosvāmīs in turn received the recognition of all followers of Caitanya. Still theirs was more a cult of Kṛṣṇa than a Caitanya cult.

In Navadvip and in Bengal generally the development of this Bhakti tradition was more in terms of a Caitanya cult. Caitanya himself was adored as Kṛṣṇa embodying in himself Rādhā also in a single personality, as he had revealed to many in his life-time. Nityānanda, whom Caitanya sent to Bengal to spread his brand of Vaiṣṇavism, himself became a deity co-ordinate with Caitanya. He was recognised as an incarnation of Balarāma. He was the first to install images of Caitanya for worship. Murāri Gupta in whose house many of Caitanya's mystic revelations in his Navadvip days took place, has left a book in Bengali called 'Kadāca', giving details of Caitanya's early life, and this became the basic text for many other successive writers like Kavi Karṇapura, Vṛndāvana-dās, Locanya-dās, Jayānanda etc. These writings all deal mainly with the details of Caitanya's pre-monastic life at Navadvip. Regarding his long pilgrimages and his thirteen years life of divine ecstasy at Puri, their treatment is in a perfunctory manner. It is Kṛṣṇadās Kavirāja's Caitanya-Caritamṛta that gives us all details about these inspiring days of his life at Puri; for he was the disciple of Gosvāmī Raghunātha Dāsa who was Caitanya's constant attendant during his life at Puri and who could therefore give him all details about that period of Caitanya's life.

All the Ācāryas of other schools of Vaiṣṇavism dealt with in this book have left very learned writings, most of them in the shape of commentaries on the important Vedānta texts and independent writings or handbooks on their doctrines. Caitanya was too God-intoxicated for this, and his renunciation began with the throwing away of his recondite writing on Nyāya into the Gaṅgā. His personal life and conversations with his disciples were the seeds from which a very varied and voluminous literature at the hands of the above-mentioned scholar disciples and devotees grew.

But Vaiṣṇavism of a kind prevailed in Bengal even long before the days of Caitanya. A king of a certain region of Bengal named Candravarman, a contemporary of Samudra Gupta (340-380), styles himself as a servant of Cakra-svāmin — a name of Viṣṇu who has Cakra or discus as one of his weapons. Many folk songs depicting the love of Rādhā and Kṛṣṇa existed, but the mass of that literature has been lost. The earliest literary composition to refer to Rādhā-Kṛṣṇa is Hala's Prākṛt work called Gītā-Saptaśati, attributed to the 2nd century. To what extent this work prevailed in Bengal cannot be ascertained. Later Vidyāpati and Caṇḍidās composed many romantic songs depicting the love between a hero and heroine, which was given a religious colour as the love of Kṛṣṇa and Rādhā. But serious literature with far-ranging implications and forming the basis of Caitanya's devotionalism, was the Bhāgavata Purāṇa in Sanskrit which is traced today to a date not earlier than the 8th century. There was also the famous composition of Jayadeva called Gīta-govindam, which is suited for singing and dancing, and which is now a musical composition recognised all over India.

Caitanya himself did not contribute any writing except the eight verses we have given towards the end. He was too God-intoxicated for any literary effort. But he introduced two important texts of the Kṛṣṇa cult that he came across during his pilgrimages. These are Līlā-śuka's Śrī Kṛṣṇa-karṇāmṛtam and Brahma-samhita which became precious texts of Bengal Vaiṣṇavism. What Caitanya did not do on the literary side, was accomplished by his learned disciples, the Vṛndāvan Gosvāmīs etc.

The Vṛndāvan Gosvāmīs wrote in Sanskrit and the others in Bengali. An Ācārya of the Vedānta is expected to write a commentary on the Vedānta Sūtras of Bādarāyaṇa. Neither Caitanya nor the Vṛndāvan Gosvāmīs had done this. This deficiency was however made up by Bāla Deva early in the 18th century by the production of such a commentary under the name Govinda Bhāṣya, which raised Caitanyaism to the full level of a Vedānta philosophy.

More important than these learned works, Caitanya's mission was fulfilled by the development of popular music, dance and devotional dramas through which the refinement of the Vaiṣṇava spirit was directly transmitted to the masses. From the very beginning of his life, his tendency was to break the rigid laws of caste and custom and cater to the needs of the poor and the depressed. In those days of illiteracy, books could benefit only a small section of the elite, but Caitanya's technique of propagating Bhakti through mass Kīrtans attended with dance and music, both vocal and instrumental, was an effective way of audio-visual education that is becoming popular in these sophisticated days. A large body of Padāvalis, which are compositions suited for recital and exposition both in Sanskrit and Bengāli, developed in the hands of talented poets like Narahari Sarkar, Sivānanda Sen and Vasudeva Ghosh and others. Innumerable folk songs of great popular appeal also came into vogue. All these made Caitanya a Deity, the embodiment of Rādhā-Kṛṣṇa, and his adoration became the religion of a very large section of the Vaisnavas of Bengal.

In concluding his account of Caitanya's life in his translation of Caitanya Caritāmṛta, Jadunath Sirkar gives the following estimate of his contribution: "Caitanya insisted on the unity of Godhead underlying the multitude of idols of popular worship. He taught that God can be realized only by means of a love ardent and all-absorbing as the conjugal passion.... His hearers were exhorted to work out their salvation, each man for himself, by strenuous holy living and not to imagine that it can be won through any other man's exertions or the mechanical performance of any ritual. Like many other Hindu reformers of medieval times he admitted all believers to his fold without distinction of caste or rank.

"But the goal of Caitanya has been lost. His Church has passed under the control of Brāhmin Gosvāmīs who have developed a very subtle and esoteric theology in which the brain has suppressed the heart. Today the Vaiṣṇava sect forms two sharply divided sections — an emotional but morally indisciplined rabble at the base and a keenly intellectual but cold and fastidious priesthood at the top, without any link between them."

# Śrī Kṛṣṇa Caitanya Philosophy

## Acintya - Bhedābheda

### Introduction

Most people generally identify Vedānta with the Kevalādvaita (Absolute Non-dualism) of Śaṅkara. While a paramount place has to be given to this system as the first systematic presentation of the Upaniṣadic teachings, the truth is that it marks but the beginning of the formulation of Vedāntic doctrines from different angles of philosophic and spiritual insight. Among the later interpretations of the Vedānta, those by the Vaiṣṇava Ācāryas (Teachers) form the most important, both from the point of view of philosophy and of the impact they have had on the religious life of the people.

Vaiṣṇava philosophers are divided into five main schools. Most of them differ from Śaṅkara, not always by denying Non-dualism as the teaching of the Upaniṣads but in their view as to what brand of Non-dualism they inculcate. The important differences may in brief be set forth thus: 1) In Śaṅkara's Non-dualism the supreme spiritual reality is the attributeless, indeterminate and acosmic Absolute. For the Vaiṣṇavas it is the Supreme Person who is the repository of all auspicious qualities and the Lord and Master of creation 2) Śaṅkara accepts God but He is distinguished from the Absolute: He is only a provisionally accepted entity who is sublated as an unreal attribution in the course of the discriminatory process. Īśvara may be the highest in the scale of relative values of the Vyāvahārika (phenomenal) plane. But everything of the phenominal plane, the lowest as well as the highest, is Mithyā (mere appearance). They sink and disappear into oblivion from the Paramārthika or the ultimately real point of view of Truth. For the Vaiṣṇavas, God is the Ultimate Reality revealed by the Vedāntic Texts, and there is no Absolute apart from Him. For, He includes everything in His being, or there is no other entity superior to Him or having independent existence beside Him. No sublation of Him in any sense is acceptable. 3) In Kevalādvaita the Jīva in its essence, i.e. after the elimination of the adjuncts of body, mind, egoism, etc., and Īśvara (God) after the elimination of His adjuncts, namely, His power of cosmic manifestation, constitute the identical non-dual Brahman. The adjuncts in both cases are unreal. For the Vaiṣṇavas the Jīva is only an aspect, part, potency or attribute of Brahman, distinguishable but not necessarily different. Some hold him to be distinct both in bondage and in salvation, while some others maintain, that the distinction will cease with liberation when the Jīva merges in Brahman as a river does in the ocean. This latter type of thinkers accept the doctrine that Upādhi or adjunct separate Jīvas from Brahman only in ignorance. The adjuncts are dissipated on the attainment of knowledge. Other schools give a distinct identity for Jīva both in ignorance and liberation. 4) For Kevalādvaita creation is unreal. If it is accepted in the Upaniṣads, it is done only provisionally, to deny its reality afterwards. For the Vaiṣṇavas creation is a real process in every sense of the term. 5) According to Kevalādvaita, Samsāra or the state of bondage and release from it, are only unreal assumptions resulting from ignorance, whereas all Vaiṣṇavas hold these to be real states. Thus, bondage is a real state and release from it is a real achievement to be had by appropriate means. 6) Jñāna or knowledge of the unity of the Ātman (self) with Brahman is the means of salvation in Kevalādvaita while the Vaiṣṇavas hold Bhakti (deep-rooted devotion and dedication to God) to be the means. 7) Release from

Samsāra or achievement of bodilessness is the goal of Kevalādvaitins. whereas service of the Supreme Being in His eternal Realm is the ideal of most of the Vaiṣṇava schools 8) Kevalādvaita is essentially a system of metaphysics with a spiritual import. Its alliance with cults and theologies is very loose, although in practice the majority of the followers of the system adhere to one. or other of the prevailing theologies as a provisional discipline. All Vaiṣṇava philosophers on the other hand, are philosophers and theologians as well, as their systems centre upon personalistic conceptions of Reality supported by philosophical structures. They are identified with certain cults.

**Caitanya School**

Among the five schools of Vaiṣṇavism, the Bengal school was inspired by the great religious teacher Śrī Caitanya who lived from 1486 to 1533. Vaiṣṇavism in a rudimentary form did exist in Bengal even before him, and the songs of devotee-singers like Caṇḍidās and Vidyāpati had already inspired the country by their thrilling compositions on Divine love. Another centre radiating Vaiṣṇava devotionalism was Jayadeva's famous musical compositions dealing with the spiritual romance of Rādhā-Kṛṣṇa mysticism. It was, however, the advent of such a mighty personality as Caitanya that gave a boost to the sect. Caitanya himself did not, however, take part directly in literary or philosophical activity. He was too full of God-love to undertake any such work. His time was spent in Divine ecstasies, in Saṅkīrtanas or singing of God's Name and excellences, and in conversing on God-love with devotees who went to him for the attainment of spiritual insight. The object of his love was Kṛṣṇa who, on the basis of certain texts in the Bhāgavata, is accepted not merely as an Incarnation of Viṣṇu but as the Supreme Godhead Himself, of whom Viṣṇu is only a partial emanation. The pattern of love popularised by him was of the conjugal form represented in the Bhāgavata Purāṇa through the love of the Gopikas of Vṛndāvan for Śrī Krsna. Though he did not write or preach any systematic philosophical doctrine, the conversations he held with devotees and disciples were in themselves profound enough for the development of a philosophy and theology centering on him. What he failed to give in writing, he made up by the impact his grand and ecstatic personality made on talented disciples. He was followed by several scholarly saints and philosophers who have presented to the world a distinctive form of metaphysics and theology that has come to be known as the Bengal school of Vaiṣṇavism or as Acintya Bhedābheda philosophy. Among these, mention must specially be made of the names of the illustrious Gosvāmīs of Vṛndāvan—Sanātana, Rūpa, and Jīva, and of Bāladeva in later times.

## II

### Its Metaphysics: The Absolute Person

The system claims itself to be Advaya Vāda, a doctrine of the one without a second, according to which Sat-Cid-Ānanda Para-Brahman, identified with Kṛṣṇa, is the one Supreme Reality. Krsna is the Absolute Person, indivisible, all-inclusive and unlimited by any other entity beside Him. He has an ideal form, the brilliance of which is what the Advaitins of Saṅkara School call the unqualified Impersonal Brahman. This is illustrated by Kṛṣṇa's statement in the Gītā "I am the support of Brahman" XIV.27. Just as the brilliance of the sun is supported by the disc of the sun, so is Brahman of Kevalādvaita which is only the Tanu-bhā, or the surrounding brilliance of the Consciousness-Bliss of Kṛṣṇa supported by Him. The epistemological theory behind this doctrine is this: That the Nirvikalpaka Jñāna (unmodified, indeterminate awareness) is the ultimate truth and that the Savikalpaka (definite awareness) is false in the last analysis, is the thesis in

Saṅkara's system of thought. The position is reversed in this system. The indefinite awareness of anything is the first and most primitive and, therefore the most peripheral, understanding of anything. When awareness becomes definite, clear and defined, then only anything is fully understood. This is true with regard to the Supreme Reality also. The Bhagavān, the Divine Personality, clear and defined, is, the core of Reality, and the indefinite and unmodified Brahman can be only His peripheral brilliance (Tanu-bhā). An Infinite Person may be a contradiction in the sphere of space and time, but it is not so in regard to Kṛṣṇa, as He is the transcendental spiritual Reality within whom time and space are included. Besides, His form is not like the forms in space and time. His is a multiform — a form which can take any other form. In Him there is no absolute distinction between spirit and form.

**Theory of Change Without Change of Substratum**

It may be asked how the non-duality of the Supreme Reality can be understood in relation to the experience of multiplicity experienced in everyday life. Every school of Vedānta has got its own answer. In Śaṅkara's system the manifold is explained away as an illusory manifestation superimposed by ignorance on the non-dual substratum. In the system of Ramanuja, the manifold is accepted as adjectively or organically related to Īśvara (God), who along with the manifold, forms the complete whole or the Absolute including in itself all that exists. In the Bengal school of Vaisnavism the relationship accepted is that of Śaktimat and Sakti, powerholder and power. An entity and its power are inseparably related and have an identity of being in spite of the difference that could be made of them. For example, fire and its potency expressing as heat and light, form an identical entity though the distinction between them is also simultaneously evident. Similar is the case with the Supreme Reality (Kṛṣṇa) and His Sakti or Potency of world manifestation. Their relationship is one of identity in difference, both the terms of the relationship being equally real. The Supreme Person remains transcendental while His Śakti projects the world of multiplicity. The multiplicity is in, and of, Śakti, and does not affect the Saktimat. At the same time Śakti, as the potency of the Saktimat, the Supreme Person, has no independent existence apart from Him and constitutes an identical Non-dual Whole with Him. Non-duality of the ultimate Reality is thus secured through the concept of Sakti which stands distinct from the Śaktimat as the source of the manifested worlds, while at the same time remaining non-different from the transcendent Śaktimat. Manifestation is real and not in any sense illusory. It is changeful, but not illusory. The Supreme Reality can have no truck with falsity in any sense.

Here the following questions will be raised: If Śakti changes in a real sense into the manifold, it must surely be affected by that change. Consequently, Śakti being one with the Śaktimat, the modification of Śakti arising from transformation must be considered as modification of Śaktimat Himself. In other words, the Supreme Reality loses its character. God ceases to be God as in all forms of Pantheism. It is to avoid this that in Śaṅkara's system of Advaita the doctrine of apparent (illusory) transformation, known technically as Vivarta Vāda as opposed to Pariṇāma Vāda (real transformation), is posited. For, when the manifold is only a super-imposition on the Ultimate Reality, that Reality, though forming the substratum of the illusory perception, is not affected by it. But this show of consistency is achieved by inconsistency in other respects. If the transformation is only apparent, this apparency must be the misreading of some one. Either it must be done by the Supreme Reality Itself or by some consciousness other than It. Non-duality precludes the existence of any other consciousness. Hence ignorance, which leads to illusion, must accrue to the Supreme Reality alone. It will thus be seen that the very defect that is sought to be circumvented, namely the corruption of the Supreme Reality by real change, recoils on this doctrinal position by loading the Supreme Reality again with ignorance. Nothing therefore is gained by this show of logic. So the Bengal School of Vaiṣṇavism rejects Māyā-Vāda and its offspring, the doctrine of Super-Imposition, and stands for the real transformation of Supreme Reality through His Śakti.

**Acintya-bhedābheda**

But the question originally posed still stands. If Śakti is identical with Śaktimat, will not the real transformation of the former be equivalent to the transformation of the latter also? In reply to this the Bengal School of Vaiṣṇavism propounds the doctrine of Inconceivable Identity-in-difference (Acintya-bhedābheda). Śakti is both identical and different from Śaktimat. It is because of this element of difference that transformation of Śakti does not affect the Śaktimat. At the same time the element of identity makes the Supreme Reality Non-dual even in the midst of difference. How these two contradictory features can co-exist is not attempted to be explained logically. For this reason it is designated as Acintya — alogical or incomprehensible by thought. It means logic, which is ultimately based on sense experience, cannot bring it within its laws and it has therefore to be accepted as a fact transcending human understanding. At the most it can be said that the idea of the cause being affected and exhausted by change, is the characteristic of relative causes bound by space and time. To apply this rule to the ultimate cause, the Cause of all causes, who has this special capacity of unaffectedness in the midst of change, is illegitimate.

To avoid admitting this inexplicability of the transformation of the non-dual Reality into the many, Kevalādvaita invokes the doctrine of apparent transformation, which lands, as shown earlier, in attributing ignorance to non-dual Reality. An attempt is made to get over this derogatory status of the Supreme Reality by claiming that ignorance (Ajñāna) in relation to the individual alone, is a disvalue. With reference to the Supreme Reality ignorance is denoted by another more dignified name. Māyā, a mysterious power of manifestation which cannot be described categorically either as Sat (existing) or as Asat (non-existing), or as Abhāva-rūpa (having only a negative entity). Māyā itself thus become Acintya (alogical and inexplicable), being both real and unreal according to Śaṅkara Vedānta. It makes Māyā a greater mystery, than Brahman Himself. The Bengal School of Vaiṣṇavism, however, points out that Māyā, being the power of the Non-dual Reality, can in no sense be unreal, and that what is Acintya (alogical and inexplicable) is the relation of Identity-in-difference between the Non-dual Reality (Śaktimat) and Māyā, its power of manifestation (Śakti) as the many. Being contradictory, their co-existence as one and the same entity cannot be understood logically. Such co-existence is however a fact of Divine life revealed by scripture and independent of any logical inference. Just like a fact of material life, for example that sugar is sweet, it does not require the support of logic. To those who still want a logical way of stating, it can be spoken of as a logical presumption (Arthāpatti), an inexplicable hypotheis, without accepting which, the non-duality of the Supreme Reality and the fact of His simultaneous manifestation as the many cannot be understood.

The advantage of this approach to the problem is that according to it life, its values, spiritual efforts, the spiritual goal of freedom etc., are accepted as factual, and the average man is thereby better placed to work for the attainment of his spiritual goal than under the gospel that seeks to overcome an actually experienced problem by denying its actuality and thus converting spiritual striving into a kind of mockbattle. Man is realistic in his outlook, and unless the means and the goal are apprehended as real, he will fail to put his best into his striving. To be told that there is no creation, no bondage, no real spiritual striving and no real liberation, will only sound a puzzle and prove a paralysing inhibition to the average man with his inborn realistic outlook. When you feel the pain of a thron that has entered into the flesh, the denial of pain will have no effect. We have to take another thorn and remove the one in the flesh, if we are to get relief.

### III

### Its Theology: Kṛṣṇa as Supreme Being

The Acintya Bhedābheda conception of Non-duality provides the metaphysical background for this school to formulate its theology. The non-dual Supreme Reality is identified with Śrī Kṛṣṇa, as revealed in the Bhāgavata Purāṇa, which is accepted by this school as the most authoritative scripture. It is looked upon as the best elucidation of the Veda. Its authority rests on the view that Vyāsa who codified the Vedas and produced the Vedānta Sūtras, himself composed the Bhāgavata in order to elucidate the abstruse meaning of the Vedic revelation. The Bhāgavata speaks of Kṛṣna as 'Bhagavān Svayam' i.e. the Supreme Being Himself. Generally in all other Hindu religious cults, Kṛṣṇa is one of the incarnations of Viṣṇu, but the Bengal School of Vaiṣṇavism makes Kṛṣṇa the Godhead and Viṣṇu one of His emanations, on the strength of the above-mentioned text. He is Sat-cid-ānanda, the Para-brahman— the Supreme Reality who is Existence-Knowledge- Bliss Absolute. But unlike in the non-dualistic Vedānta of Śaṅkara, he is the Absolute Person. Though the formless and all-pervading Brahman also is accepted, the Divine form is not a mere sublatable expression of it. The form is the more fundamental and Brahman as the formless is only His aura. He has countless forms, in fact as many as devotees care to invoke Him in, but this school accepts one form as His original and transcedental form. That is of Kṛṣṇa, the cowherd Boy of Vṛndāvān, as described in the Bhāgavata. Though the Essence of Existence, Knowledge and Bliss, He none the less bears the form of an adolescent of transcendent beauty, having two hands and feet, blue complexion like that of a fresh rain cloud, eyes resembling full-blown lotus petals, and yellow wearing clothes resembling lightning in its brilliance. Being pure Being- Consciousness- Bliss (Sat-cid-ānanda -vigraha), He has no distinction of body and soul, of form and essence. The senses and limbs of His divine form (Śrī vigraha) too are not to be differentiated from His essence. They have nothing in common with the material organs of human beings. A material form can be only in one place at a time, and it is identical with itself and different from others. But the form of Kṛṣṇa is an all-inclusive multi-form, which can appear as Kṛṣṇa, or in any other form, in all places simultaneously. Not only His two-handed form but His dress, His residence, His playmates like the cowherds and cowherdesses are all eternal forms without any material limitations and can appear anywhere to the eyes of a devotee on whom He bestows His grace. This two-handed form of Kṛṣṇa has been revealed to sages who have attained to the required stage of purification and resignation. It will still be reveald to kindred spirits. It has therefore to be accepted as factual and not a mere subjective fancy.

## The Formful Higher than the Formless

The reasoning behind the acceptance of a form as the Supreme Reality has already been given. The formless, changeless, indefinite and all-pervasive and attributeless intuition of the Absolute represents only a peripheral understanding just like the initial, vague apprehension of an object (Nirvikalpaka-jñāna). Definiteness being the sign of clarity and completeness of understanding, the intuition of the Supreme Person with an ideal form of Bliss-Consciousness represents a core understanding of Reality. For Kṛṣṇa, who is Pure Spirit, form is no limitation as it is for material objects. He is the central core of Existence. Knowledge-Bliss, of whom the unmodified Nirguṇa Brahman is the all-pervading brilliance, just as limitless light is of the condensed essence of its source, the sun. Kṛṣṇa again is Rasa — Bliss or Mādhurya (Sweetness) — with Aiśvaryas (majesties) suppressed and obscured by it. Mādhurya is the highest value, Aiśvarya (majesty) comes only after that. So those who adore the very core of the Supreme Reality practise devotion to Kṛṣṇa as all-sweetness (Madhurya), and not to His Aiśvarya aspects represented by Paramātman, called also as Vāsudeva, Nārāyaṇa etc. These Aiśvarya aspects, which are only partial revelations of Kṛṣṇa, form the object of adoration in several other schools of Vaiṣṇavism.

They are not, however, different from Kṛṣṇa, but His partial manifestations, with Aiśvarya predominating and Mādhurya, the highest spiritual value, as only subsidiary, Kṛṣṇa, however, embodies all the Bhagas, the sixfold Divine majesties of Aiśvarya (power), Dharma (goodness) Yaśas (glory), Śrī (splendour), Jñāna (knowledge) and Vairāgya (detachment), for which reason He is called the Bhagavān. But over and above all these, He is pure Bliss, of which there is only a partial expression in His aspect as Paramātman and much less in Brahman, the formless, indeterminate and pervasive spiritual aura of His. It is on this ground that the followers of this school of thought maintain that the Brahman-intuition of the Advaita Vedānta is an initial step in which spiritual aspirants are stranded if they are not properly guided by the Bhakti Sāstra. The authority quoted for this gradation of the Supreme Being into Brahman, Paramatman and Bhagavān as the progressive and hierarchical structure of the Non-dual Reality is the Bhāgvata Verse: "What the truth-knowers call the Non-dual consciousness, even that is spoken of as Brahman, Paramātman and Bhagavān" (Bg.1-2-11).

## Krsna And His Threefold Śaktis

It has already been pointed out that the Non-duality of the Supreme Reality, Krsna, is sustained with the aid of the conception of His Śakti or Potency of manifestation which stands to Him in the relationship of inconceivable identity-in- difference. Śakti is not different from Him, just as the burning property of fire is not from fire. Śakti effects all transformations while Kṛṣṇa remains unaffected, as the transcendent and immanent presence supporting Śakti.

Śakti has three aspects — Svarūpa Śakti (Innate Potency), Taṭastha Śakti (Peripheral or marginal potency, also called Jīva Śakti or (Jīva Potency), and Bahiraṅga Śakti (Extraneous Potency). Bahiraṅga Śakti is the power of cosmic manifestation. The cycles of creation (Sṛṣṭi) and dissolution (Pralaya) of all the fourteen spheres, as also of the gross and subtle elements which constitute these spheres and the bodies of Jīvas inhabiting them, spring from the transformations of this last mentioned Śakti. It is called Bahiraṅga or extraneous because it is insentient gross matter (Prakṛti) constituted of the three Guṇas of Sattva, Rajas and Tamas, and only the attribute of Sat (existence) characteristic of the Supreme Reality is seen to be manifest in it. So though, as His Śakti, it is one with Him, it is devoid of Consciousness (Cit) and Blissfulness (Ānanda) that form the core of His Being. It is based on Him only indirectly, and its transformations do not affect His transcendent Being in any way. For this reason its relation with Him is extraneous, in contrast to that of His Svarūpa Śakti (Inherent Potency of Bliss). Being thus of the nature of self-alienation, it is also called Māyā Śakti. But the term Māyā in this system carries no significance of illusoriness as in Śaṅkara's Advaita Vedānta. It is a real power inherent in the Supreme Reality, and all its effects are real. But it binds Jīvas (centres of consciousness) in materiality and makes them forgetful of their Divine affinities. It is the Lord's power by which the process of creation is originated and sustained. In contrast to it stands the Lord's Redemptive Power known as Cit Śakti, which, being the same as Svarūpa Śakti, will be discussed under that concept.

Subtler than the Māyā Śakti of the Lord and closer to Him in relationship is the Jīva Śakti, also called Tatastha

Śakti. It is constituted of the countless centres of Consciousness called Jīvas (life monads) who are expressions of His attribute of Consciousness or Cit. The Jīva, in this system is an Energy or Potency of the Lord, His power of self-multiplication, just as matter is His power of material evolution. It is called Taṭastha (literally meaning 'situated on river bank'), because just as the bank of a river links the liquid waters with the dry land and partakes of the characteristics of both, the Jīvas too, as centres of consciousness, stand between, and partake of the nature of, the two other Powers of the Lord — His material power known as His Māyā or Bahiraṅga (extraneous) Śakti on the one hand, and His spiritual power called Cit, or the Antaraṅga (inward), or Svarūpa (inherent) Śakti, on the other. Being in contact with both, the Jīva gets into the state of bondage (Samsāra) when Māyā Śakti dominates over him and makes him purely body-minded, but when through the practice of devotion and the grace of the Lord, the Jīva is enfolded by the Svarūpa Śakti (the same as Cit Śakti) of the Lord, he attains to his higher spiritual evolution.

The Jīva in this system is not equated with Brahman (Non-dual Reality), but is regarded as both identical and different from Him. The Jīvas in their totality form His Jīva Śakti, and it is one with Him in the sense that Śakti (Power) and Śaktimat (Power-holder) are one and not different. Each Jīva, however, is an intelligent subject corresponding to the 'I' sense and retains his individuality through all changes occurring in physical embodiment. It is self-luminous (Svayam-prakāśa), conscious (Cetana), subject to ego-sense (Ahamartha), different in different bodies (Pratyak-kṣetra-bhinna), atomic, (Aṇu), ever-pure (Nitya-nirmala), a centre of knowledge, action and enjoyment, and endowed with a natural tendency towards Paramātman. Though it is called atomic it should not be conceived as a material atom, as it is not subject to spatial measurement. The expression is used to indicate that it is an individuation of Divine Power and has its distinctiveness as a monad. Just as the sparks thrown out by a fire share its nature in a fragmented condition, so also the Jīvas embody a very limited quantum of the Bhagavat's nature as Existence- Knowledge- Bliss. But they are never identical with Him either in bondage or liberation. They are His dependants, related to Him as His Taṭastha Śakti (peripheral potency). Though the Jīva, coming under the influence of Māyā Śakti, forgets his spiritual nature and gets identified with materiality, he never loses his essential spiritual attributes. They only get contracted in the state of ignorant identification with the body under the influence of Māyā. When the obstructing veils of Māyā Śakti are removed through Bhakti (devotion), they become sharers of the blissful nature of the Svarūpa Śakti of the Bhagavat. But they always retain their individuality even in liberation and become Parikāras or attendants of the Lord in the hierarchy of the spiritual world. They may lose their sense of individual existence in the bliss of Divine communion but this does not mean that their distinctive entity is lost.

## Svarūpa Śakti in the Three Aspects

The third and most fundamental potency of the Bhagavān is called Svarūpa Śakti, meaning innate or essential potency. It is also known as Antaraṅga (inward) in contrast to Bahiraṅga (extraneous) Śakti, and as Cit (Spiritual) in contrast to the same Śakti as Māyā (material) Śakti. While all these three Śaktis mentioned are based on the Bhagavat and have no existence apart from Him, the first two are peripheral in different degrees to Him: it is only the Svarūpa Śakti that is directly associated with Him. The other two, Māyā (Bahiraṅga) and Jīva (Taṭastha) Śaktis, are displayed by Him only indirectly in His role as the Paramātman who, as mentioned earlier, is a partial expression of Kṛṣṇa, embodying only his Aiśvarya (Lordliness) but not His Mādhurya (Sweetness or Blissful nature). Māyā functions under the direction and control of the Paramātman, while the Svarūpa Śakti of the Bhagavān transcends the working of Māyā. The Jīva Sakti, too, is directed by the Paramātman while it is in its embodiments in material nature and therefore allied to Māyā then; but, as stated earlier, through Bhakti it breaks the hold of Māyā and comes under the influence of Svarūpa Śakti. It is because of its intermediate situtation and status that it is called marginal (Taṭastha).

Svarūpa Śakti has three aspects known as Sandhinī, Samvit, and Hlādinī, corresponding to the Supreme Being as Sat (Existence), Cit (Consciousness) and Ānanda (Bliss). Sandhinī, corresponding to the attribute of Sat (Existence), is the energy of the Lord by which He sustains His own existence as also of the Jīvas and the worlds. Samvit, corresponding to Cit (Consciousness), is His knowledge-nature by which He has self-knowledge and also knows others and endows others with knowledge. Hlādinī, corresponding to Ānanda (Bliss), is the energy by which He enjoys His own innate Bliss and makes others enjoy the same. Just as the psychological and physical formations of the material world are formed by the combinations of the aspects of material Prakṛti known as Sattva, Rajas and Tamas, the manifestations of Svarūpa Śakti in different degrees and combinations constitute the stuff and energies of the spiritual dimension. It is called Śuddha Sattva, self-luminous and untainted spiritual element, as distinguished from ordinary material Sattva forming an aspect of Māyā Śakṭi along with Rajas (dynamism) and Tamas (inertia). Material Sattva is tainted with Rajas and Tamas and is not self-luminous. It is subject to change and limitations of space and time. Śuddha Sattva is the opposite of this and knows no limitations and has no taints. It is the subtlest, immaterial energy of Intelligence and Bliss. When Sandhinī predominates, Śuddha Sattva expresses itself as Ādhāra Śakti—the root energy which manifests as, and sustains, the Heavenly Residence of the Bhagavat. The dominance of Samvit generates the manifestation of Śuddha Sattva called Ātma Vidyā or self-knowledge which sustains all forms of spiritual consciousness. When Hlādinī predominates over the other elements, the spiritual energy expresses itself as Guhya Vidyā or pure loving devotion (Prema Bhakti).

Of all the three Śaktis, the Svarūpa Śakti is the most intimate and fundamental nature of the Bhagavān, and of the three aspects of Svarūpa Śakti, Hlādinī, the energy of Bliss, is its essence. The scriptures have described the Supreme Reality, Kṛṣṇa, as Rasa which means the same as Ananda or Bliss. The concept of Bliss becomes meaningful only when it is a matter of self-realisation or realisation in an object. To speak of Brahman as Bliss in the sense that it is without sorrow, as certain philosophers do, is meaningless, because even a stone, being without sorrow, can be described as bliss in that sense. Bliss without self-awareness and awareness of the others is meaningless and indistinguishable from mere inertness. So Srī Kṛṣṇa, the Supreme Reality, is not only Rasa but also Rasika, the enjoyer of Bliss. He is an enjoyer in two ways — both in His identity with, and in His difference from, His energy of Bliss (Hlādinī), which is the essence of His Svarūpa Śakti. Self-enjoyment of Himself as Bliss is called Svarūpānanda of enjoyment in identity. Distinguished from this is His enjoyment of His own Potency of Bliss (Hlādinī), which is known as Śaktyānanda; for, as His Śakti, Hlādinī, is both identical and different from Him. Hlādinī the essence of His Svarūpa Śakti, is therefore personified as a Female, Rādhā, forming the counter-whole and Eternal Consort of Kṛṣṇa. The Supreme Reality is therefore represented as Kṛṣṇa embraced by Rādhā. The function of the Śaktis of Kṛṣṇa is to carry out His will and contribute to His sportive manifestations, which form the expression of His essential nature as Bliss. The whole of the cosmic manifestation and withdrawl is a sport which He performs through His Bahiraṅga (extraneous) Śakti, known also as Māyā. Basically it is like a dance or circular movement of electrons round a nucleus, and of planets and galaxies round a central source of attraction. The evolution of life and the progress of the soul in higher regions is His sportive manifestation through His Jīva Śakti, also called Taṭastha Śakti. The recurring cycles of Samsāra that carry Jivas through repeated births and deaths until emancipation, is the dance of sportive Kṛṣṇa at the level of this intermediate Śakti.

**Goloka the Supreme Abode**

The blissful and sportive nature of Kṛṣṇa is most conspicuously manifest in His eternal dance with his Svarūpa Śakti in the transcendental realm of Goloka. The other Śaktis, though basically dependent on Him, are not directly in communion with Him. They are under the direction of His lower manifestation described as Paramātman whose abode is the Vaikuṇṭha. Paramātman is the expression of Aiśvarya (majesty), whereas Kṛṣṇa, the Supreme Reality, is in addition Mādhurya (Sweetness or Bliss). The energy of Bliss, Hlādinī, alone is in direct communion with Him. The Hlādinī, as it has already been stated, is personated as Rādhā who is engaged in eternal service of Kṛṣṇa, thus affording Him what is called Śaktyānanda, the realisation of His own Bliss through the service rendered to Him by of His Śakti(Hlādinī). Rādhā who is His Svarūpa Śakti, and therefore the foremost of His Servitors, expands herself into thousands of Gopis. Rādhā and her Gopis have no thought of self and form the highest expression of perfect self-effacement through their loving service of Kṛṣṇa. As His Śaktis, the purpose of their existence is this self-effacement in His service.

Rādhā invariably approaches Kṛṣṇa in the attitude of Mahābhāva, the perfect sentiment of love. The exuberance of their joy takes the form of the choral dance of Rādhā and Kṛṣṇa surrounded by the countless Gopikas dancing in pair with Kṛṣṇa-counterparts into which He multiplies Himself. This ecstatic dance of numerous pairs in circle is called Rāsalīlā. The Jīvas who adore Kṛṣṇa through pure

Bhakti are graced by His Svarūpa Śakti and lifted out of the domain of Māyā and made participants of the Bliss of Goloka where the eternal dance of Kṛṣṇa with Rādhikā and the Gopikas is going on.

Goloka, otherwise known also as Vṛndāvana and Mahāvaikuntha, is the transcendental Abode of Kṛṣṇa formed of Suddha-sattva for His residence by his Svarupa Śakti. There Kṛṣṇa is eternally manifest in the form and dress of a Gopa or cowherd along with Rādhā, His counter-whole, and His Parīkāras or retinue of attendants consisting of Gopas and Gopikas. They all, in a sense, constitute the structure of Kṛṣṇa in so far as they are the formations of His Svarūpa Śakti, which is none other than Rādhā herself. As expressions of His Śakti, they minister to Him with absolute love and dedication without any touch of self-centred objectives. They set the standard for the Jīvas pursuing the path of devotion as to how Kṛṣṇa is to be served with loving dedication. Every Jīva, irrespective of his male or female embodiment, is a Śakti of Kṛṣṇa, being a part of his Taṭastha Śakti (Marginal Power) also known as Jīva Śakti. Only overpowered by Māyā, he is forgetful of this truth until by the practice of Bhakti he is liberated from the hold of Māyā and comes under the influence of Svarūpa Śakti, who, as Hlādinī, rouses in Him the sense of right relationship with Kṛṣṇa and draws him to the life of Bliss consisting in the selfless service of Kṛṣṇa in Goloka otherwise known as Vṛndāvana.

## The Unalloyed Purity of Rādhā-Kṛṣṇa Conception

The teachers of this school are never tired of warning their students of their devotional literature against the possible misconception that the relationship of Kṛṣṇa with His Śakti has a sexual basis. Sex is something physical pertaining to the biological life of creatures on earth. It is included in physical nature which is a part of Māyā Śakti. Even the Jīva, which is included in Taṭastha Śakti, has no sex in Itself, but it acquires it, when it identifies itself with the physical body under the influence of Māyā Sakti. But Vṛndāvana and its denizens are all the expression of Svarūpa Śakti, and everything there, including the bodies of the Parikāras of Kṛṣṇa, are formed of Suddha-sattva (unsullied stuff of Spiritual Consciousness), which has nothing to do with the combinations born of Sattva, Rajas and Tamas, the constituents of material Prakṛti. Hence the description of Goloka is the very antipode of sex-life. Sex is based on physical body and is motivated by self-centred pleasure. Love is self-giving, but sex is absolutely self-regarding. At the human level there is a certain intermingling of these two — a sugar-coating of an absolutely brutal physical instinct with a pure spiritual value. The love that is evinced in the Parikāras of Kṛṣṇa is not to be understood in terms of this worldly love. Perhaps it may be correct to understand worldly love at its best as a distorted reflection of that value in its pristine purity as it manifests in the Parikāras of Kṛṣṇa. That love is without the slightest touch of self-centredness. The little self is forgotten in the joy of serving Kṛṣṇa, and pleasure and pain look alike when they are related to His service. The happiness of Kṛṣṇa becomes the sole reward and motivating force that His servitors know of. The joy of Goloka is the expression of the Hlādinī Śakti, Kṛṣṇa's power of Bliss, and a participant of it must necessarily have shifted his centre from the narrow little self to the Sat-Cid-Ānanda, the All-comprehensive Divine Person.

It is also to be noted that this school uses the terms male and female in a mystic sense. Kṛṣṇa is the only Male, and His threefold Sakti is considered Female in relation to Him. Thus all embodied beings, irrespective of whether they have male or female bodies, are expressions of the Śakti and are Female in the mystic sense attached to this term. It is also contended that contemplation on the blissful dance of Kṛṣṇa with His Śakti in Goloka, instead of making man sex-minded, will cure him for all time of this weakness, the universal ailment of all mankind.

## Emanation of Kṛṣṇa

Goloka, the supreme Abode of Kṛṣṇa, is said to transcend all the worlds born of Prakṛti and the abodes of all divine manifestations. The fourteen material worlds are ensheathed by eight Āvaraṇas (covering layers), and the whole is encircled by the transcendental ocean called Kāraṇa Samudra or Viraja (literally meaning Causal Ocean or that which is beyond Rajas). Siddhaloka, the region of Nirguṇa Brahman, is beyond this ocean. Transcending it is Parmavyoman, the abode of the partial manifestation of Kṛṣṇa known also as Narayaṇa, Paramātman etc. Māyā Śakti is directly under the control of Nārāyaṇa or Paramātman, who is the manifestation of Kṛṣṇa's majesties (Aiśvarya nature) as contrasted with His blissfulness (Mādhurya). All the incarnations except Kṛṣṇa come from this Paramavyoman. Goloka, also known as Vṛndāvana, transcends this heavenly abode also. There, in that region of Light and Bliss, Kṛṣṇa, in the simple but most enchanting form of a Gopa, is served by His Parikāras, and is engaged in His eternal Rāsa Dance.

The eternal Goloka is non-phenomenal but Krsna manifests Himself with all His Parikāras in the earthly Vṛndāvana. He and His associates are present in two ways. He is also present there in an unseen way. This is called His Aprakaṭa Prakāśa or unmanifest appearance. But He also descends on it in a manifest form, perceptible to the eyes. This is Prakaṭa Prakasa, and is called Pūrṇāvatara, His complete and perfect Incarnation. In this sense it is that this school holds that Kṛṣṇa is the only full Incarnation, and all others are Amsas or partial manifestations of Narayaṇa.

IV

## Bhakti as the Way of Higher Spiritual Fulfilment

Theology and metaphysics are not ends in themselves in this system as also in others. It is a means to help man in attaining the spiritual summum bonum. The essential means for this is Bhakti, which may be translated as loving and adoring service of God. The word Bhakti comes from the root Bhaj which has several meanings, many of them being purely secular. In the devotional sense it means complete loving servitude or Seva, and so Bhakti has been described by Nārada Pañcarātra as whole-hearted loving service of the Supreme Being without any other consideration than the joy of the beloved Lord. It springs from the consciousness that the individual soul or Jīva, being part of God's Śakti as described in the earlier section, finds its meaning and fulfilment in dedication to, and service of, Him. Under the influence of Avidyā the Jīva identifies himself with matter and is engrossed in physical enjoyments, which the Māyā Śakti offers. But sufferings and a sense of futility in life turn the Jīva away from these material engrossment in course of time and prepare him for receiving the message of Bhakti. This message comes through contact with holy men, from whom one hears about the Lord's excellences. Passing through various preparatory disciplines, the Jīva realises that as the Prakṛti of the Lord, he is not a self-existent entity but an eternal dependant and servitor of His, and that he can find his self-fulfilment only in cultivating loving and self-less service of Him. This way of life as a monadic fraction of the Lord, wherein the interest of the Jīva is shifted from his individual self to the Spiritual Whole and finds fulfilment in entire submission and loving service of Him, is Bhakti.

Bhakti in this sense is an end in itself. It is to be distinguished from Mukti or liberation, which is generally put as the fourth and the highest value of life. Mukti is union with the Supreme. A Jīva, by following the path of Jñāna or knowledge can get merged in Brahman-consciousness and thereby gain Mukti. But Brahman is only the Tanu-bhā or the peripheral lustre of Kṛṣṇa as has already been pointed out, and to be merged in that is to be deprived of the supreme felicity of love and service of Kṛṣṇa, which is looked upon as a distinct fifth Puruṣārtha (value of life) by this school following the teachings of the Bhāgavata. A follower of this school of Vedānta is therefore asked in the beginning itself to eschew Mukti and its Sādhana called the path of Jñāna (knowledge) which leads to the dissolution of individuality in the Divine, thus making it impossible for the Jīva to attain love and service of the Divine, which form the highest possibility open for him. For, the ideal condition in the eyes of the Bhakta is not to become sugar but to taste it.

So also the path of Bhakti has no element of Karma in it. Karma here means Vedic ritualistic actions either of an obligatory nature or of an optional nature, for attainment of heavenly enjoyments. Promises of such rewards held forth in the Veda are only Parokṣa Vāda — a bait held out to unregenerate minds so as to bring them into the path of God ultimately and are not to be understood literally. Vedic rituals are therefore to be eschewed, and in their place, specific devotional rituals forming part of the Bhakti discipline, are to be adopted. But discharge of one's duties in selflessness and detachment and as an offering to God, has a place in the devotee's life, as it leads to purification of his mind through the elimination of the Āsuric (demoniac) tendencies born of self-centredness. Thereby it increases the competence of the aspirant to follow the specific Bhakti disciplines. But then such Karma is a part and parcel of Bhakti discipline and should be distinguished from the pursuit of Vedic Karma.

The path of Yoga or concentration may be considered an independent path leading the Jīva to the Paramātman, the intermediate aspect of the Divine as the seat of all power and glory. Just like the path of Jñāna, this also is a diversion from the goal of the highest felicity that is Bhakti. But the methods of concentration adopted by the Yogins can be usefully employed in the path of Bhakti also as an aid to hold the mind in concentration on the Lord.

Bhakti is thus independent of all other Yogas. It is both the end and the means, and the term Bhakti is often used indiscriminately to indicate both these aspects. As an end, it is the highest goal of the Jīva, and consists in the experience of pure delight (Prīti) in the service of Kṛṣṇa without any thought of any extraneous objective like Moksa or attainment of any object of desire obtainable by human effort. Thus as an end, it is an attitude and an experience, while as a means it is a set of specific disciplines. Sādhya Bhakti and Sādhanā Bhakti are the two technical terms used to indicate this difference.

## Vaidhī or Sādhanā Bhakti

Sādhanā Bhakti or disciplinary devotion is divided into two stages - Vaidhī Bhakti and Rāgānugā Bhakti. Vaidhī Bhakti means practice of the set of rules and disciplines laid down in Bhakti texts with a view to stimulate the feeling of love for God with the help of external aids, while the Rāgānugā is the highest stage of these disciplines in which external aids are minimised and this stimulation is accomplished more by psychological means. A man may be said to be fit for practising Vaidhī Bhakti when deep faith (Śraddhā) in a spiritual reality has dawned on him. Till then also a man may be following what is called Sādhanā Bhakti or devotional observances in a conventional way, but that is more a matter of routine and social conformity. Śraddhā is generated in the mind of man by association with holy men whose conduct and conversations alone can impress a person with the existential nature of the spiritual reality. Hence association with holy men is the most important factor in the generation of devotion. A person with Śraddhā launches on the practice of devotional disciplines, which have been elaborated into sixty-three as follows: 1) submission to the Guru; 2) receiving; initiation and lessons from him in the devotion to Kṛṣṇa; 3) serving the teacher; 4) following the conduct of saints; 5) inquiry into what is true religion; 6) abstinence; 7) living in sacred places of the Vaiṣṇavas; 8) earning only for maintenance and not hoarding; 9) observing fast on Ekādaśi etc; 10) respecting Sālagrāma and other emblems of Viṣṇu; 11) keeping away from atheists and impious men; 12) avoiding making too many disciples and getting entangled in their affairs; 13) avoiding too many ambitious projects; 14) avoiding writing too many books, practising too many crafts, delivering too many lectures, and involvement in too many disputations; 15) giving up faulty behaviour; 16) not being overwhelmed by adverse fortune; 17) avoiding disrespect to the Deity as worshipped by others; 18) not harassing others; 19)&20) avoiding Sevāparādha (disrespectful behaviour in worshhip) and Nāmāparādha (disrespcet to Divine Name); 21) intolerance of criticism of Kṛṣṇa and His devotees; 22) putting on the Vaiṣṇava marks; 23) stamping the letter 'Hari' on the arms: 24) accepting with devotion flowers, Tulasi etc., offered to the Lord; 25) dancing before the Deity; 26)&27) prostrating before the Deity and the Guru; 28) following the Deity in religious processions; 29) circumambulating the Deity in the temples; 30) going to the temple regularly; 31) worshipping the Deity regularly; 32) serving the Deity in all possible ways; 33) singing the praise of Kṛṣṇa; 34) performing Sankīrtana (collective singing); 35) silently repeating the Divine Name (Japa); 36) revealing one's innermost feelings to the Deity; 37) repeating devotional verses; 38) eating with relish what is offered to the Deity (Prasāda); 39) drinking the water with which the Deity is washed; 40) smelling the fragrance of flowers, incense etc., offered to the Deity; 41) touching the Deity; 42) Gazing at the Deity; 43) witnessing the evening and other services at the temple; 44) listening to the recitation of the names of the Lord (Sahasranāma etc); 45) seeking the Lord's grace; 46) remembering the Lord always; 47) meditating on the Lord; 48) adopting the attitude of servant towards the Lord; 49) adopting a friend's attitude towards the Lord; 50) dedicating oneself to the Lord; 51) offering to Him all that is dear to oneself; 52) using all one's energies towards performing His work; 53) absolute self-surrender; 54) tending Tulasi plants etc., associated with Him; 55) following the scriptures; 56) residing in Mathura and other holy places; 57) serving the devotees (Vaiṣṇavas); 58) holding devotional festivals according to one's capacity; 59) observing monthly vows especially in Kārtika; 60) observing Janmāṣṭami with special reverence; 61) loving the feet of the Deity; 62) studying the Bhāgavata Purāṇa with fellow devotees; and 63) maintaining contact with Bhaktas more evolved than oneself.

This long list is more or less the elaboration of the nine limbs of devotional discipline described in the Bhāgavata as consisting in Śravaṇa (hearing the excellences of the Lord), Kīrtana (singing His praise), Smaraṇa (remembering Him by repeating His Name), Pādasevanam (service of the world as God's manifestation), Arcana (worship of Him in holy images), Vandana (obeisance to Him), Dāsya (feeling of being His servant), Sakhya (having intimacy of friendship), and Atmanivedana (dedicating oneself wholly to Him). But there are three items that are new. First of all there is the step of accepting a Guru. This is necessary, because though God is the only Guru ultimately, we get His guidance chiefly through human agencies. Either a holy man or the Head of an Order representing a spiritual tradition is approached by a disciple for spiritual initiation. Holy formulae of Divine name combined with Bījas, transmitted from generations of Gurus to disciples, are communicated to the initiates. These Mantras are potent with spiritual power, and through devoted and concentrated repetition of these and meditation on their meaning, the spiritual power of the disciples is developed. The teacher who initiates is called Dīkṣā-Guru and he can be only one. In addition, one can have a Sikṣā-Guru who teaches ways of worship; chanting and other spiritual practices. Mention is made also of a third type of Guru known as Caitanya-Guru whose function is to impart the esoteric meaning of the sacred Mantras and various practices and procedures involved in worship. A competent Guru can, however, fulfil all these functions. Service of the Guru occupies a very important place in the discipline. It is as important as the service of God Himself, since it is only by the grace of the Guru that spiritual efforts will fructify.

In the list given, mention is made of what may be described as devotional offences, Sevāparādha and Nāmāparādha. Sevāparādha (offence relating to worship) consists in failure to observe the rules of purity, procedure and reverential homage in one's association with temples of God and worship of holy images. Some of these include moving about irreverently before holy images, indulging in impure or prohibited practices in temples, not contributing according to one's capacity for worship, eating without offering to the Lord, offering from what has been eaten already etc. Nāmāparādha is disrespect shown to the Divine Name which is as weighty and holy as God Himself. Ten such offences are enumerated; slandering saintly persons; regarding the Name and attributes of Śiva as independent of those of Viṣṇu; ignoring spiritual preceptors; finding fault with scriptures; taking the praises of Divine Name found in scriptures as exaggerations (Arthavāda); deliberately sin, or resolve to sin, with the idea that one can absolve oneself from them later by chanting the Divine Name; holding an attitude of indifference to Divine Name; considering oneself superior to the Divine Name; and imparting the Divine Name to people who have no faith in it.

## Rāgānugā Bhakti

By the long and sincere practice of Vaidhī Bhakti, in which the attempt is to stimulate the sense of loving adoration of God with the help of external aids, the devotional sentiment becomes more and more natural, and a devotee is then considered fit to practise the next stage called Rāgānugā Bhakti. The expression means the attempt to imitate and thereby generate in oneself, the Rāga or loving attachment that manifested in the various Vṛndāvana associates of Kṛṣṇa in their relation with Him. Here also there is an external aid but it is of the nature of imaginative concentration through impersonation. In the life of Śrī Kṛṣṇa at Vṛndavana and Mathura he is found to entertain different forms of loving relationship towards different devotees who were the earthly manifestations of His eternal Parikāras (attendants). The Bhāgavata declares that Kṛṣṇa is the Beloved, the Soul, the Son, the Friend, the respected Ancestor, the Relative and the desirable Deity. He appeared as the beloved (Priya) to the Gopis and His queens; as the soul (Ātmā) to ascetics like Sanaka; as the son (Suta) to Nanda and Yasodā; as the friend (Sakhā) to Gopas like Sūdāmā; as respected ancestor (Guru) to Pradyumna and others; as loving well-wisher (Suhṛt) to Arjuna and like-minded friends; and as the Chosen Deity (Iṣṭa Deva) to Uddhava and other devotees like Him. Now the devotee who practises Rāgānugā Bhakti is to live in imaginative identification with any of these associates of Kṛṣṇa representing the attitude he is practising, and thereby produce in himself vicariously that Bhāva or devotional attitude manifested in the relationship of that Vṛndāvana associate of Kṛṣṇa. The Bhāvas or devotional sentiments that could be cultivated are five: Śānta (peaceful), Dāsya (servitor's), Sakhya (friend's), Vātsalya (parental), and Mādhurya (conjugal). The Sānta Bhāva is generally discarded by the followers of this system, as it is suited only for those who consider Jñāna and Mukti (knowledge of oneness and liberation) as the goal. They are the votaries of Brahman or Paramātman aspects of the Supreme Reality, Kṛṣṇa. The object of such devotional practice is freedom from Samsāra through mergence in His being. But Kṛṣṇa in His essence as Mādhurya (Sweetness, Bliss) can be attained only through Bhakti of the highest order known as Prema or Prīti, which is realised in service of Him and not in mergence. The essence of this form of Bhakti is the acceptance of the sentiment that Kṛṣṇa is one's own (Mamatā-bhāva) and the consequent forgetfulness of His majesty in an overwhelming sense of His dearness. The intimate personal relationships like those of a servant, friend, parent and sweet-heart provide channels for the expression of this kind of loving devotion (Prema Bhakti) to Kṛṣṇa when the devotee has come to recognise Him as his 'Own', the nearest and the dearest. The life of Kṛṣṇa as described in the Bhāgavata is unique for the depiction of these forms of love through the experiences of His Parikāras (associates and attendants) mentioned earlier. One practising Rāgānugā-bhakti is to gain imaginative identification with one or the other of these Parikāras and participate vicariously in their loving relationship and service of Kṛṣṇa. Devotees of this type, in order to get full identification, are asked to spend as much of their time as possible at Maṭhura and Vṛndāvana, where Kṛṣṇa's earthly manifestation took place. Even the dress and ways of life associated with the Parikāra impersonated and the Bhāva contemplated on, are enjoined to be adopted by the practising devotee.

The adoption of Rāgānugā- Bhakti does not require the abandonment of the discipline of Vaidhī Bhakti like hearing the scriptures, chanting the Divine Name, serving teacher etc. mentioned earlier, but there is a decided shift to inner factors like contemplation for stimulating the sentiment of loving relationship.

**Prema Bhakti**

When the sense of intimate relationship with Kṛṣṇa has become natural and continuously sustained even without any external aid, it is said to have become Rāgātmikā (of the very nature of attachment) in contrast to Rāgānugā (of the nature of imitation). Devotion is then said to have transcended the Sādhanā (disciplinary) stage and attained to the Sādhya (accomplished) stage. It is also given the descriptive name of Prema Bhakti (loving devotion) or Prīti (the sense of dearness and delight in respect of God). Prema or Prīti becomes possible only when one has learnt to feel that God is one's 'own' (Mamatā-bhāva). Forgetting His power and majesty as creator, preserver and destroyer, one has to be established in any relationship of love with Him mentioned before and be habituated to look on oneself as Kṛṣṇa's servant, friend, parent or sweet-heart. Only in such intimate relationships can one feel Him as one's own. Each of the above mentioned forms of love is included in the succeeding one, and the last of them, namely, the relationship of the sweet-heart, therefore includes all others in it and marks the acme of divine love (Prema). The classic example of such love is the love of the Gopikas for Kṛṣṇa described in the Bhāgavata, and it is the aspiration of every devotee of this school to be blessed with at least a little of this form of intense God-love in their heart.

Prema-bhakti, on its first manifestation, that is, before it has deepened, is called Bhāva. Bhāva is called the morning sun of Prema, announcing the emergence of a new factor into the life of the devotee. Though the Sādhanā Bhakti might have prepared the mind, Prema cannot be called a mere product of the preparatory disciplines. It is an expression of Kṛṣṇa's grace and is called a special manifestation of Śuddha-sattva. An expression of Kṛṣṇa's Svarūpa-Śakti, Hlādinī or His inherent Potency of Bliss, is cast on the devotee, and it is the reflection of Hlādinī from the devotee's heart in the form of love and service that is called Prema, to which Bhāva stands as the dawn stands to day. The efflorescence of this form of love has certain characteristics. Internally the devotee begins to feel an intense engrossment with the Lord (Rati) from which his mind refuses to move. As a result he develops a liquidity and smoothness of the heart. He is established in a state of placidity of mind (Kṣānti), in which he could remain unperturbed by all circumstances that ordinarily cause cares, anxieties and disturbances. He spends all his time in devotional mood and practices like chanting the Divine Name, hearing the exposition of His glories and excellences etc. He evinces no interest in or attraction for objects of the senses. His conviction in the possibility of realising the Divine becomes unshakably established due to the fore-taste of it got in Bhāva.

Bhāva deepened is called Prema or supreme love of God based on an apprehension of Him as the dearest. It is also called Prīti or the joy of unselfish love and service. The joyous experience of this type is to be distinguished from Sukha or happiness and satisfaction. Happiness can be a purely self-centred satisfaction derived from a self-centred pursuit. But in the joy that is called Prīti, there is no pursuit of pleasure for one's own sake; there is only the thought of service and happiness of the beloved Lord in complete forgetfulness of oneself and one's own welfare.

Such self-forgetting dedication, uncorrupted by the narrow self, eliminates from the aspirant all thoughts of attaining Mukti, or release from the cycle of birth and death, even if this might follow as a consequence of the dawn of pure devotion. A true Bhakta (devotee) does not care for it even if this fulfilment called the fourth Puruṣārtha is offered. He seeks only liberation into the joy of serving God who is Joy. One who has attained this state of mind is said to have attained the fifth Puruṣārtha the state of selflessness.

Prīti does not involve any personal effort, but flows easily through God's grace. It manifests when devotional attachment takes a purely personal form as a servant's to the Master, a friend's to a friend, a parent's to the child, or a woman's to a lover, and results in intense attraction to the Lord. But it is pointed out that Prīti involves no sensual attraction, though the language and the symbolism used to describe the attraction, deprivation and satisfaction involved in it may take an erotic form. For selflessness, as already pointed out, is the characteristic of spiritual love, whereas self-consideration is the very basis of sensuous attachments.

It is through Prīti alone that the most unique aspects or nature of the Lord is revealed. He is characterised by the basic quality of 'belovedness' which is revealed only to the eye of love. Philosophic apprehension can grasp Him only as impersonal and changeless substratum or as omnipotent creative power. Aspirants who do not follow the devotional discipline of love and service but seek for unity (knowledge) and liberation (Mukti), attain to these lower aspects of the Supreme Being known as Brahman and Paramātman. The intellectual intuition of the Impersonal Brahman, of which Śaṅkara's Advaita speaks, is according to this school, only absorption in the Sat (existence) aspect of Kṛṣṇa. The impersonality and relationlessness of this intellectual intuition (Jñāna) in which Śaṅkarites see the special excellences and superiority of their system, are viewed in the reverse manner by this school as the precursor of the concreteness of the transcendent experience of Kṛṣṇa as the object of love. What is presented in Brahman-intuition is only the generic aspect of the concrete spiritual reality. Savikalpaka, distinguished by clearness and definiteness, is the characteristic of the core of Reality, while the Nirvikalpaka, the boundless and the relationless, is only its peripheral aspect. Only Bhakti, love-consciousness, opens the path to this transcendent experience of God as Bliss (Ānanda). But even in Bhakti, if the outlook of the devotee is dominated by the consciousness of the power and glory of the Divine, the devotee can attain only to Paramātman, otherwise known as Nārāyaṇa, Ādiviṣṇu etc. but not to the Bhagavan (Kṛṣṇa), of whom Paramātman and Brahman are only aspects. It is only to the devotee who abandons even Mukti and loves Kṛṣṇa for the sheer joy of serving Him that He reveals His most supreme attribute of 'belovedness' (*priyatva-lakṣaṇa dharma-viśeṣa*), which is the essence of His power of Bliss (Hlādinī). Prīti is thus the experience of loving God and being loved by Him. The Lord is immersed in two distinguishable variations of Bliss. He is of the substance of Ānanda Bliss. But Ānanda to be significant, should be conceived also as enjoyable. Sugar is by nature sweet but sweetness is revealed only when it is tasted. So the blissful Bhagavān becomes the enjoyer of Bliss (Rasika) through His potency of Bliss which is technically called Hlādinī (identified with Rādhā) which manifests as His form, associates, the Gopas and Gopikas, residence etc. Of all these manifestations of Hlādinī, devotion of the nature of Prema is perhaps the most unique. Hlādinī flowing out into the Jīva, transfigures him into a poem of love and service directed towards the Lord, creating in the latter the thrill of responsive love (Śaktyānanda) that reveals His own essential nature of belovedness to Himself through the Jīva. Thus the Lord becomes dear to devotee and the devotee becomes dear to the Lord, generating the unique thrill of Bliss in both. It is therefore said in the Bhakti texts that the Lord is overpowered by the love of the devotees and has subordinated Himself to them. "Being a lover of my devotees", He says in the Bhāgavata, "I am subordinate to them. My heart being in the hold of my devotees, I am as it were, one without freedom." In the Gītā also He declares: "The Jñānī (meaning the devotee of the highest type), who is ever in communion with Me and has exclusive love of Me, excels over all. I am the dearest to the Jñānī, and he is dear to Me. While all types of devotees are noble, the Jñānī is considered by Me as My very self' (Gita VII, 17&18).

**Stages of development of Prīti**

The progress of Bhakti as Prīti (i.e. as distinguished from disciplinary devotion). is divided into seven stages. (1) Rati or Bhāva is marked by natural attachment and absorption in the Lord without the need of any external stimuli (2) Prema is the indissoluble attachment binding the devotee to God by the sense of 'myness' (3) Sneha is the end product of Prema when the heart melts in love. (4)

Māna is marked by sensitiveness due to excessive love. (5) Rāga is eager longing for the object of love touched with the enjoyable pain associated with it. (6) Anurāga is the experience of unceasing novelty in the object of love. (7) Mahā-bhāva is the most ecstatic expression of love, and is called Divyonmāda (Divine madness). The savants of Caitanya School enumerate about twenty characteristics, physical and psychological, as expressions of this unique Divine sentiment in both its phases as love in union and love in separation. Some of these unique characteristics are: intense longing, inability to bear separation, readiness to bear even intense pain in the interest of the beloved, loss of the sense of time, power to influence one's environment with the intensity of one's feeling, loss of sense of self even in normal consciousness, loss of all fear of death and welcoming it as the means for elemental union with Kṛṣṇa, supra-normal behaviour that looks like 'Divine madness' and so on.

Mahā-bhāva is said to have manifested only in the Gopikas and in some Divine Incarnations like Śrī Caitanya and Śrī Rāmakṛṣṇa. The God-love of devotees will ordinarily rise to the state of Rati or Bhāva only, but not Mahā-bhāva. According to the identification they establish with the Parikāras of Kṛṣṇa, only partial manifestations of Divyonmāda (frenzy of divine love) may appear in them. But once Rati is established in the mind of a devotee, God's grace generates in Him Prema (self-abnegating love expressing itself in service), and it reveals to him God as the Beloved, the centre of all love and attraction. In the words of the Bhāgavata Purāṇa, he becomes a Bhāagavatottama who "sees the glory of God in all beings and all beings as resting in God."